RECKONING WITH COLIN ROWE

While the first half of the twentieth century in architecture was, to a large extent, characterized by innovations in aesthetics (accompanied by succinct and polemical manifestos), the postwar decades saw emerge a more refined and intellectual disciplinary framework that eventually metamorphosed into the highly theory-focused moment of the "postmodern." Colin Frederick Rowe (1920–1999) was a leader of this epistemic shift due to his aptitude to connect his historical and philosophical erudition to the visual analysis of architecture.

This book unites ten different perspectives from architects whose lives and ideas intersected with Rowe's, including:

Robert Maxwell
Anthony Vidler
Peter Eisenman
O. Mathias Ungers
Léon Krier
Rem Koolhaas
Alan Colquhoun
Robert Slutzky
Bernhard Hoesli
Bernard Tschumi
With an introduction by Emmanuel Petit and a postscript by Jonah Rowen.

In their critical assessment of a key twentieth-century formalist, these renowned architects reflect on how their own positions came to diverge from Rowe's. *Reckoning with Colin Rowe* is a thought-provoking discussion of key schools, places, concepts, and people of architectural theory since the postwar years, illustrated with over forty beautiful black-and-white drawings and photographs.

Emmanuel Petit studied architecture at the ETH in Zurich, Switzerland, and received his PhD in history and theory of architecture from Princeton University, USA. He has taught at Yale, USA; Harvard, USA; and the Massachusetts Institute of Technology, USA, as associate professor and visiting associate professor, respectively; and is currently Sir Banister Fletcher Visiting Professor at The Bartlett School of Architecture in London, UK. He is author of *Irony, or the Self-critical Opacity of Post-modern Architecture* (2013).

RECKONING WITH COLIN ROWE

Ten Architects Take Position

Edited by Emmanuel Petit

Routledge
Taylor & Francis Group

NEW YORK AND LONDON

First published 2015
by Routledge
711 Third Avenue, New York, NY 10017

and by Routledge
2 Park Square, Milton Park, Abingdon, Oxon OX14 4RN

Routledge is an imprint of the Taylor & Francis Group, an informa business

© 2015 Taylor & Francis

Library of Congress Cataloging-in-Publication Data

Reckoning with Colin Rowe : ten architects take position / [edited by]
Emmanuel Petit.
   pages cm
Includes bibliographical references and index.
1. Rowe, Colin. 2. Architecture, Modern—20th century.   I. Petit, Emmanuel,
1973- editor.   II. Maxwell, Robert, 1922- Mannerism and modernism.
   NA2599.8.R69R43   2015
   720.92—dc23   2014032743

ISBN: 978-0-415-74154-5 (hbk)
ISBN: 978-0-415-74155-2 (pbk)
ISBN: 978-1-315-81525-1 (ebk)

Acquisition Editor: Wendy Fuller
Editorial Assistant: Grace Harrison
Production Editor: Ed Gibbons

Typeset in Bembo
by Apex CoVantage, LLC

Printed and bound in the United States of America by
Edwards Brothers Malloy on sustainably sourced paper

CONTENTS

ACKNOWLEDGMENTS

The idea for this book was launched in 2000—one year after Colin Rowe had passed away—at the initiative of Alan Colquhoun and Peter Eisenman. Alan and Peter wanted to illustrate how Rowe had spawned a myriad of very different theoretical positions as a reaction to his own theses in architecture; they detected that I had a vivid interest in the hypotheses of formalism, and thus asked me to gather this collection of essays.

All texts are original contributions with the exception of Bernhard Hoesli's; unlike Jim Stirling and John Hejduk, who I would certainly have asked to write essays had they still been alive, Hoesli had written an explicit response to Rowe before he died in 1984; I reprinted the "Addendum" from his *Transparency*, which the Institute for the Theory and History of Architecture (gta) at the Swiss Federal Institute of Technology (ETH) in Zurich had first published in 1968. I thank De Gruyter for permitting the reprint of this text. Anthony Vidler's essay is a revised and much expanded version of his "Up Against the Wall: Colin Rowe at La Tourette," published in *Log* 24 (Winter–Spring 2012): 7–17. Robert Slutzky's text is the result of a series of conversations, which I recorded and transcribed in Elkins Park, Pennsylvania, in 2002, before he passed away in 2005; these interviews were later edited to their current form by Joan Ockman. O. Mathias Ungers and Alan Colquhoun died in 2007 and 2012, respectively, but had given me their essays a few years earlier.

This book is made possible with the support of the Yale School of Architecture and especially the generosity of Robert A.M. Stern, Dean. Further support comes from the A. Whitney Griswold Faculty Research Grant from the Whitney Center for the Humanities.

I thank Jonah Rowen for his witty and efficient help with the book as assistant editor, and for writing the Postscript. Thanks also to Robert Somol for interviewing Rem Koolhaas about Rowe in Los Angeles in 2002 and for transcribing the conversation for the book and to Eduardo Vivanco for his help with the book in earlier stages of its production.

I thank Routledge and Wendy Fuller, Emma Gadsden, and Grace Harrison for making this collection of texts available in the form of a book, and for guiding me through the maze of the world of publishing.

The editor and publisher gratefully acknowledge the permission granted to reproduce the copyright material in this book. We thank Fondation Le Corbusier, Galerie Strecker, Rosa Feliu Atienza, Richard Bryant, Arcaid, Artists Rights Society, Centro Internazionale di Studi di Architettura Andrea Palladio, Massimo Listri, Courtauld Institute of Art Gallery, Architectural Review, The Provost and Fellows of the Queen's College in Oxford, Cemal Emden, OMA/AMO, Spiegel, MIT Press, John Hill, Peter Eisenman, Ungers Archiv für Architekturwissenschaften, Archives d'Architecture Moderne, Léon Krier, Ralitza Petit, Burcin Yildirim, Canadian Centre for Architecture, Joan Ockman, Miroslava Brooks, Mark Jarzombek, and Archives Bernard Tschumi for granting permission to reproduce the images in the book. Every effort has been made to trace copyright holders and to obtain their permission for the use of copyright material. The editor and the publisher apologize for any errors or omissions in the preceding list and the credits and would be grateful if notified of any corrections that should be incorporated in future reprints or editions of this book.

Last but not least, I thank the contributors for their willingness to share their genuine interest in architectural concepts: Alan Colquhoun, Peter Eisenman, Bernhard Hoesli, Rem Koolhaas, Léon Krier, Robert Maxwell, Robert Slutzky, Bernard Tschumi, O. Mathias Ungers, and Anthony Vidler.

E.P., New Haven, Connecticut, July 2014

Portrait of Colin Rowe (February 1980)

Credit: © Rosa Feliu Atienza, Barcelona

Introduction

ROWE AFTER COLIN ROWE[1]

Emmanuel Petit

Multi-Perspectivalism

I experienced Colin Rowe only once, at the Swiss Federal Institute of Technology (ETH) in Zurich in June 1997—two years before his passing—when he spoke as the éminence grise on the occasion of the 30th anniversary of the Institute for the History and Theory of Architecture (gta); the date also coincided with the 50th anniversary of the first publication of "The Mathematics of the Ideal Villa" in *Architectural Review*. I have to confess that even though I was an advanced student of architecture at the time, his talk struck me as arcane. I remember that his rhetoric appeared very unorthodox for the Swiss academic context we were accustomed to: he structured his lecture around two slides, one of which showed the garden facade of Palazzo Farnese at Caprarola and the other one, a page of Bill Watterson's strip cartoon *Calvin and Hobbes*. While the Villa Caprarola image and the paired slides in the tradition of Wölfflin and Giedion felt familiar for a lecture in architectural theory, the cartoon was decidedly not.

It is in hindsight that I reconstruct Rowe's reason for bringing up the cartoon. As is well known, this graphic novel narrates the adventures of six-year-old Calvin and his stuffed tiger Hobbes; while all the grown-ups see Hobbes as a mere inanimate toy, to Calvin's imaginative mind, he is a live tiger and dynamic play companion. The cartoon characters are allegedly named after the 16th-century French Reformation theologian Jean Calvin and the 17th-century English political philosopher Thomas Hobbes. I had assumed that Rowe wanted to show how inert matter and static form come to life in the imagined interaction between the ideas from divergent intellectual spheres and historical times—just like what he, himself, had argued with Palladio and Le Corbusier. Only in this case, it was the historical figures of Calvin and Hobbes: whereas the former one concerned himself with ideals of thought (metaphysics), the latter focused on action (politics). Those were the essential poles around which Rowe's own view of the ideals of modernity was organized; considering it an impossibility to make the developments in aesthetic and political form coincide, Rowe decided that it was opportune to concentrate on the "enjoyment of utopian poetics without . . . the embarrassment of utopian politics."[2] I had concluded that the little boy, Calvin, might have abided by this sort of credo when his inanimate play companion made him do all sorts of outrageous things, and that, accordingly, his political skills with his parents were not to be considered his forte.

A search in the gta archive revealed, however, that Rowe brought up the cartoon strip for another reason: in the particular episode he discussed, Calvin just comes out of a dispute with his father, who urges his offspring to try to see *both sides* of the issue. As a reaction, Calvin promptly envisages that both his bedroom and he, himself, are all of a sudden subjected to a neo-cubist transformation that allows him to see all perspectives at once. Immersed in this complex and contradictory formal world, Calvin ascertains that "the multiple views provide too much information! It's impossible to move!"[3] Calvin then set his mind to work very hard to return his bedroom, Rowe explained, "to what approximated his ideas of Renaissance perspective." Rowe subsequently disagreed with Calvin's deep attachment to a "single-minded and simple-minded world" and further ascribed the boy's attitude to a particular genre of American wit: "like most people everywhere in the world, the Americans entertain terribly banal thoughts. But since there are so very many of them, prominent displays of wit do sometimes surface. And there have been some bitter and slightly mad eruptions of brilliance, which I suspect are among the products of a disappointed puritanism, which is often both devastating and endearing."[4] Rowe was an American citizen by the time of this lecture, and he certainly enjoyed the double vantage point he occupied from the two sides of the Atlantic—as a Brit and an American. The notions of multi-perspectivalism and non-literalism, which he mostly extracted from the lessons of Analytic Cubism, remained constant epistemological givens for Rowe, from the early to his later essays—from "Transparency: Literal and Phenomenal" to *Collage City* and to *Architecture of Good Intentions*. Just as much as he stuck to certain principles when conceptualizing visual phenomena, the antagonist worldview stayed constant as well throughout the years: the technological and zeitgeist biases, or teleological historicism, which see certain trends and tendencies as unavoidable, self-propelled, and inexorable, and which anticipate a future time when all tensions will be resolved. To contrast Calvin's preference for all things literal, simple, and clear, Rowe then elucidated in his lecture the complex *double entendre* of phenomenal transparency inherent in the facade of the Villa Caprarola; furthermore, he rehearsed his tenet that architecture can only emerge in the interaction between historical knowledge and visual literacy, which he saw as the brick and mortar of the discipline of architecture.

At the risk of succumbing, myself, to what Rowe might well have construed as a zeitgeist argument, I want to suggest that between Rowe's last lectures and texts in the 1990s and today, architecture and architectural theory have evolved considerably, and so have both the technological and cultural grounds of formalism. In fact, mine is not so much a zeitgeist argument—a notion to which cling all the implications of technological progress and Hegelian *Aufhebung* ever since the particular spin given by the rhetoric of the modern movement—as it is simply a point concerning the changing cultural episteme.

In Rowe's time, the circuits of architectural theory were mostly triangulated between London, Venice, and New York—an exchange between Europe and the United States, which historiography recorded as an extremely intense and fruitful episode of architectural culture. Today, the geographical map of architecture has become broader and more heterogeneous; therefore, a retreat into the same disciplinary frontiers of architecture and architectural theory than the ones drawn up by Rowe would be restrictive.

Two lines of investigation of the transformation of the episteme are key to the present condition of formalism, which Rowe would have had to address had he still been writing today. The first one relates to the development of philosophical attitudes toward the city, history, and the question of meaning in architectural theory—especially with regard to the new urban developments in the Near and Far East; the other one partly emerges from the former and pertains to the technological and conceptual retooling of the architectural design process. Whereas the former evolution reveals Rowe's worn Eurocentrism, the latter has made it increasingly difficult to conceptualize "disciplinarity," as Rowe did, without pondering the new technologies of form generation and representation, and uncovering an alternative history of precedents for this context. It is worthwhile staking out the field of this recent evolution of theory in architecture before letting the contributors to this book account for how they helped prepare the grounds for it; each one of them intersected with Rowe's ideas and initially used them as a stepping-stone, only to then resolutely swerve from his ideological orbit and create new concepts for the discipline.

New Urbanisms

The narrow selection of specifically theory-minded architects in this book notwithstanding, Rowe's ideas were appropriated by a whole ideological spectrum of architects, who based their pursuits on very divergent deontologies. In particular, two opposed ideological factions would loosely claim ties to Rowe's legacy: it is remarkable and perplexing that, in the United States, both the formal experiments out of the (neo-)avant-garde and the neoconservative attitudes toward the city, could each be traced back to Rowe and his entourage. The stakes of the different groups in this discussion can be worked out in the philosophical distinction between the notions of architectural drawing versus diagram—between the iconographic content of the drawing and the formal immanence of the diagram.

One of these groups made itself an outgrowth of the urban turn of early postmodern architectural theory, and hoped to base the rules for a new urbanism on principles of the traditional city. The roots to this series of interests are multiple, and include intellectual trends on both sides of the Atlantic; in Europe, they include the critique of Team X, Neo-Rationalism, the Tendenza, Léon Krier's and O. Mathias Ungers's urban proposals, and Aldo Rossi's *Architecture of the City*, among others. In the United States, the conceptual antagonism between Rowe and Vincent Scully encapsulated the polemics about the right ideology for the late-20th-century city. Scully's analyses principally focused on architectural iconography based on U.S. references—such as Jane Jacobs's reverence of Main Street in *Life and Death of Great American Cities*, the New England vernacular styles, and ultimately on Robert Venturi's work. Notwithstanding shared interests in the cultural content of architectural form, Rowe's studies differentiated themselves from Scully's in that they were committed to a certain flat abstraction, where the plan was seen as the key medium through which to think architectural and urban ideas. The influence of Le Corbusier's maxim *"le plan est le générateur"* determined Rowe's methodology of spatial analysis in the city. And the notions of "figure/ground" and "contextualism" had first transpired in Rowe's Urban Design Studios at Cornell as recurring and active concepts of urban design.[5] Rowe was surrounded by Tom Schumacher, Franz Oswald, Fred Koetter, Jerry Wells, Steven Peterson, Judith DiMaio, Alexander Caragonne, and others, with whom he developed urban projects that combined in a collage the advantages of two major urbanistic conceptions—of the traditional city, on one hand, and the modern city in the park, on the other.

Rowe's own understanding of what constitutes "complexity" of architectural and urban space shifted throughout the years: in the mid-1950s, he extracted a very different space conception from Analytic Cubism than he did in the 1970s. Both of Rowe's key conceptual notions—"transparency" and "collage"—were extracted from the perceptual and conceptual logic of cubist art in relation to Gestalt psychology; for that reason, the flat plane of vision was always of primary importance to his understanding of architecture. However, when Rowe turned the argument of the transparency of form from the vertical plane (of his architectural analyses) into the horizontal plane in order to develop a theory for urbanism, he stopped using the term *transparency* and instead spoke of *collage*—yet nowhere did Rowe address the critical difference between the two notions.[6] The swap of one critical term for another had significant consequences for his outlook and divided his work into an earlier and later period. Indeed, not all collages hinge on phenomenal transparency in Gyorgy Kepes's sense—that is, the interpenetration of figures without optical destruction of each other; collages are mostly based on formal ruptures and on the tearing of paper and the side-by-side gluing of incongruous geometries and figures. Unlike the conceptual device of transparency, collage involves the more classical rules of pictorial composition.[7]

At the time of *Collage City*, Rowe became more concerned with the question of how the geometry of the city could negotiate the adjacency of heterogeneous and conflicting demands (of the modern and the traditional city) than he was with the formal intricacy produced by the mechanism of phenomenal transparency per se. And whereas Rowe related his rapprochement of traditional and modern urban paradigms to the moderate humanisms of Karl Popper and Karl Mannheim, Scully had independently worked to build a humanist historical lineage for the architecture of his time, from Hadrian's villa to Venturi's Mother's House—as he did in his *American Architecture and Urbanism* from 1969. The difference between the two versions of humanism is essential for what was to follow: Rowe never assumed that a static or synthetic stance of humanism—encapsulated in the concept of utopia—was either possible or desirable to realize: he saw utopia as a reality-transcending attitude that is inherently unrealizable. Furthermore, he found the creative engine of architecture in the dialectic between the order of the traditional city and the dynamic logic of modern urbanism: utopia as a directive instead of as an achievable state of being. By comparison, Scully's view of the city was conciliatory and based on the assumption that the urban texture was a place of harmonious and quasi-sacred integration of the divergent forces of history; his view was backed up by references to the transcendentalist philosophies of Henry Thoreau and others.[8]

In the United States, the disenchantment with postwar urban renewal was profound, and so the neoconservative approach to context became very popular; unlike the more abstract urban reconstruction efforts of the Neo-Rationalists in Europe, the American contextualists integrated concepts of town planning with the stylistic characteristics of traditional townscapes. For this, they readily appropriated Rowe's figure/ground studies as the central technique of their new urbanism centered on the primacy of the street space and found in pattern language in the tradition of Christopher Alexander a method to give order to the seeming disorder of urban structures. The concerns with the urban grammar directed at integrating the idiosyncrasies of individuality with the order of the collective, were supplemented with arguments about the phenomenology of American townscapes. Andrés Duany and Elizabeth Plater-Zyberk made themselves the principal codifiers and popularizers of the so-called New Urbanism, and defended street-based town planning as a new civic art. In 1993, they cofounded the "Congress for the New Urbanism," which published its Charter of the New Urbanism in 2000. In this context, the architectural drawing stands in as the signifier of a traditional approach to the formal expression of urban space centered on the scale of the human being. Combining the conceptual progenitors of both the contextualism in Rowe's Cornell studios and of Scully's study of American towns and architecture, the New Urbanists have integrated these principles into the pragmatism of sustainable building and town planning codes and standards—always connected to static and conservative views of humanism, about which Rowe remained critical.

Despite Rowe's explicit rejection of any instrumentalist view of architecture, expressed in the "critical" ruptures produced by urban collages, his compositional attitude toward urban design and his belief in the existence of a small number of architectural *partis*, encouraged a reactionary stance toward urban modernization not so different from the one defended by the New Urbanists. Looking back from the perspective of the current, 21st-century discussions about the massive urbanization in the Near and Far Eastern countries, Rowe's urban paradigm displays all the symptoms of a worn Eurocentrism that feels romanticizing. In fact, the global export of a definition of the "discipline" of architecture grounded in European, as much as some European-derived American history, has already produced the most awkward effects on cities throughout the world; many of Rowe's Italianocentric views have been presented as universal principles by both Rowe himself as well as his students.

Herein, collage was the *Über*-principle, which would facilitate the tolerant coexistence of dissonant spatial paradigms in the city. Yet collage hinges on the notion of the overall arrangement of a canvas and was invented as an artistic mechanism to preserve the psychological integrity of the "modern" subject in a world that started to lose its coherence—and to deal with the shock of encountering the disorder of the modern city. European cities could profit a lot from the idea of a historically informed contextualism—as for example the International Building Exhibition (IBA) in Berlin proved in the 1980s; this is for the reason that a rich palimpsest of historical layers could be found in Berlin and that the wounds of the World Wars and the Cold War were deep and visible. The ruptured and torn fragments of a collage are part of constructing a larger, consistent identity—such as the unified character of a "city." But this is exactly where Rowe's paradigm seems to have lost the battle against the zeitgeist: the sheer quantity of manifold interests and ideologies in the ever-expanding "global" cities in a largely neoliberal political climate, simply do not offer the standpoint from which a comprehensive urban composition can be organized—even in Europe. Instead, many of the new cities hinge on the simple side-by-sidedness of individual structures—often at the scale of singular buildings and building groups; regardless of how one wants to evaluate the merit of such a new urban condition, Rowe's artistic notions of figure/ground and *poché* appear out of place with regard to today's actual politics of private ownership, limited public land control, and decentralized and international decision making. Also, the forced invocation of an historical consciousness and identity in urban places, which do not have a long history (or any history for that matter), has produced a worldwide proliferation of kitsch and Disneyfied versions of the contextualist city.

At Cornell, Ungers had challenged Rowe's use of the cubist logic to conceptualize the city, and replaced it with the "unreason" of the surrealist collage of René Magritte: surrealism radically undermined the part-to-whole relationship that was so central to cubism—making thus possible an unmediated and sometimes absurd side-by-sidedness of unrelated elements on a canvas. Additionally, the rules of the surrealist drawing technique of the *cadavre exquis* fundamentally allowed for a multiple and nonhierarchical authorship without the need for formal unification and mediation (in the form of poché, for instance). Today, Ungers's project "City in the City—Berlin, the Green Archipelago," which he had developed during a Cornell summer academy in 1977 with the help of Rem Koolhaas, Peter Riemann, Hans Kollhoff, and Arthur Ovaska, has gained new currency for the reason that the scheme eschews the need for a unifying vision for the city, and instead, is based on the very coexistence of juxtaposed or antithetic urban units.[9] Looking at the current developments in cities from Dubai to Shanghai, such a co-location of individual urban miniature cities seems like a conceptual precondition to absorb the heterogeneous demands of today's cultural and economic contexts. Koolhaas kept developing this approach when he claimed in the mid-1990s that "[t]his century has been a losing battle with the issue of quantity. . . . If there is to be a 'new urbanism' it will not be based on the twin fantasies of order and omnipotence; it will be the staging of uncertainty. . . . Liberated from its atavistic duties . . . urbanism can lighten up, become a Gay Science–Lite Urbanism."[10] Lite Urbanism was directly addressed against the metaphysical views of Rowe at a time when the pervasive and increasing diversity of cultures in today's urban agglomerations make Rowe's culturally based theories look *recherché*, or quite simply incomprehensible even to those who inhabit the city.

In 2004, German philosopher and Nietzsche interpreter Peter Sloterdijk suggested a reading of the contemporary urban environment, which questions Rowe's contextualism in ways similar to Koolhaas's notion of urbanism as a gay science. Against Rowe's focus on the metaphysical and historical charge of the urban plan, Sloterdijk maintains that human ontology is to be conceptualized as fundamentally spatial and volumetric and that the assumption of a collective cultural horizon has to be replaced with a hypothesis, where humans inhabit individual spheres;[11] he further implies that the volumetric dimensionality of Being is to be transposed into the way we fathom the human habitat: as a sort of "foam" structure where individuals can indulge in "co-isolation" in their respective spheres, and are liberated from the gravity of a common history. He points out the difference of his conceptual framework with previous models of modern and postmodern urban theory, when he explains that foams are "more interdependent and connected than an archipelago but less dense than the so-called masses or crowds."[12] While the notion of "masses" implicitly refers to the *Grossstadt* theories of Walter Benjamin and Siegfried Krakauer, and is arguably instantiated in the expansive diagrammatic structure of Ludwig Hilberseimer's Berlin Grossstadt project, the structure of the "archipelago" intimates both Ungers's and Rowe's fragmentary urbanisms. Sloterdijk offers a way into understanding the urban physiognomy of the global *Individualgesellschaft*, which is tentatively implied in urban conditions like the skyline of Shanghai-Pudong—despite the political system it has emerged from. In Shanghai, the complexity of the vertical forms and zoning (as if several cities were stacked on top of one another at variable scales) seems to transcend any of Rowe's theories of urban architecture; the latter's horizontalism (even when extruded into the third dimension) needs to be updated with a theory of the volumetric. The new digital tools make such a changed conceptual approach to the city more probable than was the case in Rowe's time.

Rowe did not face the realities of massive urbanization and global communication that only started to emerge at the time of his death—when cultural heterogeneity became the normalcy rather than the occasional and mysterious manifestation of the "other," and when the myth of modern progressivism, which he so vehemently opposed, had waned. By the end of the century, Western cities routinely absorbed those patches of modern urbanization, and so the idea of a collaged city lost its operational gist and became simply descriptive of the status quo even though its fragmentary aesthetic slowly turned rearguard.

Toward the Immanence of Form and Projective Form

The second group who built on Rowe rejected the stable humanism of neoconservative town planners, and maintained that Rowe had offered architecture a different kind of disciplinary philosophy, which transcended both the do-good-ist, pragmatic, and experience-based methods of both the new urban conservatives *and* the liberated, go-for-broke approach of Lite Urbanism. The notational device of the diagram, which Rowe had inherited from Rudolph Wittkower as one of the key conceptual devices to navigate the space of history, became a major battlefield for the 1980s' and early 1990s' discussions of poststructuralism and "textuality" in architecture, from Bernard Tschumi to Peter Eisenman. The diagram undermines the iconographic and representational dimension of the architectural drawing—including its subservience to external preconceptions about a more ethical world and technological progress, and substitutes it with an internalized, self-reflexive, speculative, and self-referential formal reality. In other words, it is the structure of transparency—not collage—which underlies the diagram. The connections between Rowe and this moment of architectural history are well known, not least from Eisenman and Greg Lynn, who very explicitly articulated the differences between Rowe's "ideal" versus their own "virtual" diagrams; while Rowe articulated the existence of an ideal mathematics of architecture, the latter defined in their own ways the diagram in terms of a sheer multiplicity, where the order of ideality gets replaced with the multiplicitous and unstable state of virtual notations.

The early 1990s were a time when the theses of poststructuralism underwent major transformations in that the privileged metaphor in the humanities shifted from text to body and from meaning to affect and sensation—an intellectual realignment, which Rowe never wished to follow. And yet the outcome of this turn most radically called into question Rowe's metaphysical model of architecture, according to which form acquired its signification and attributes in relation to a culturally developed disciplinary knowledge.

Among the symptoms of this change, the Whitney Museum in New York City exhibited two shows in 1993, which were based on a particular aspect of the body that effectively challenged the theses of formalism in art: "Abject Art: Repulsion and Desire in American Art" and "The Subject of Rape" related imagery associated with the fragmented, decayed, and the taboo body to American feminist theory, European Surrealist theory of Georges Bataille, and Julia Kristeva's psychoanalytic study of the notion of abject in Powers of Horror. The aesthetic categories related to the scatological, necrophilia, mortality, and devious sexuality suggested that the study of signs and of the expressive or meaningful body had given way to a vitalist streak in art and philosophy. *October* magazine held a roundtable on the topic of abjection and the related notion of the formless in 1993; this event included Benjamin Buchloh, Yve-Alain Bois, Hal Foster, Rosalind Krauss, and Denis Hollier, among others.[13] In 1997, Bois and Krauss published *Formless: A User's Guide*, in which they explored ideas for the understanding of art outside of any formalist reification of matter and inscribed in a most radical ontology of becoming; they related form to notions of performance and action, such as the visual and functional mutations of bodily fluids. In the context of this interest in vitalist thought, a wider range of Nietzsche interpreters became directly relevant again for art and architecture theory, including not only Bataille but also Michel Foucault, Gilles Deleuze, and Félix Guattari and—mostly owing to Deleuze's work on the philosopher of intuitive and immediate experience—Henri Bergson. Bois's and Krauss's "fake" dictionary of new art historical concepts was published by Zone Books, which had also released three Bataille and three Deleuze book translations in just one year, from 1991–92; they also issued a series of books on the history of the human body, edited by Michel Feher, Jonathan Crary, and Sanford Kwinter, and dealing with the biotechnical convergence of the once distinct worlds of the machine and the organism—of the biosphere and the mechanosphere.[14]

A year before Deleuze's death in 1995, Deleuze and Guattari's manifesto *What Is Philosophy?* on philosophical creativity was translated into English; in it, the philosophers particularly discussed the relationship between notions of percept, affect, and concept. And just prior to this, in 1992, Deleuze's study of the painter Francis Bacon from 1981 was translated. The influence of *Francis Bacon: Logic of Sensation* on the formalist discussion in architecture can barely be overestimated: Deleuze made a case that Bacon's painterly form was irreducible to linguistic, historical, and cultural structures of meaning, narrative, and representation. Instead, Deleuze paid attention to material, "marks that are irrational, involuntary, accidental, free, random, non-representative, non-illustrative, non-narrative."[15] The basis for the forms, which emerge from such a materialist field of relations, could not have registered on Rowe's cerebral and cultural radar. Indeed, in comparison to Rowe's, the workings of Deleuze's diagrams are far more transformative of the source forms on which the diagram operates. In addition, Deleuze's diagram does not derive its energy from its placement in a semiological context, but from its intrinsic material conditions—or conditions of "immanence." Deleuze explains that the creative process "starts with a figurative form, a diagram intervenes and scrambles it, and a form of a completely different nature emerges from the diagram, which is called the Figure."[16] Deleuze's two-partite structure of the diagram (figurative form/scrambling) resembles Rowe's at first (parti/historical transformation), but then, unlike Rowe, Deleuze's mechanism allows for non-intellectual, affective realities to interact with linguistic structures, and transform them to a point where the symbolic value of the initial source figure is obliterated.

By the 1990s, the field of architectural theory was well prepared to participate in this affective turn of the humanities, on which Rowe chose not to comment although it represented a most potent critique of his ideas. Tschumi had already appropriated Bataille's theory of eroticism in the 1970s to challenge the metaphysical reification of form; Koolhaas and Ungers had looked to surrealism (Dali and Magritte, respectively) to question the rational grounds of modernism and its history; Anthony Vidler had written on the romantic notions of the *unheimlich*, the sublime, and the haunted house in the mid-1980s. In architectural discourse, the influence of Deleuzianism transpired most visibly in Anyone Corporation's books and conferences as well as in a series of essays the magazines *ANY, Architectural Design* (*AD*), and *Assemblage*.

In the early 1990s, *AD* started to embrace the inception of digital design culture in architecture and the formal intricacies associated with blobs, biomorphism, and algorithms. Amongst the many issues of the magazine that dealt with the intersection between computational architecture and many of Deleuze's philosophical notions—such as rhizomatics, the fold, the objectile, the smooth versus the striated, immanence—Greg Lynn guest edited the 1993 issue *Folding in Architecture*, in which Deleuze was put center stage for offering new spatial models of complexity over the previous, fragmentary collage aesthetics, which Rowe had promoted. In *Assemblage*, Deleuzianism became increasingly pronounced toward the end of the 1990s, mostly with contributions by Georges Teyssot (in relation to the notion of difference), Michael Speaks (action and pragmatism), Arie Graafland (rhizome), Lynn (body without organs), and Sylvia Lavin (affect), among others. Already from its launch, *Assemblage* had emerged from a context that was explicitly Deleuze-inspired, as it was given its name in reference to the philosopher's theory of *agencement*—a French term initially known in the English-speaking world as "assemblage theory." The notion of assemblage added an anti-structuralist concept to its sister terms of *collage, bricolage*, and *montage*, to which the discipline was partly introduced by Rowe and Koetter's postmodern urban manifesto *Collage City*. By the last issue of *Assemblage* in 2000, it was clear that architecture could no longer be thought of "as an isomorph of the categories and operations of theory"[17] and that the foundation for architectural form was not chiefly to be found in either the formalist idealism of the early Rowe texts, or a focus on historical antecedents of the later Rowe.

Among these magazines, *ANY* had emerged amid the architectural discussions about textuality and Derridean deconstruction and slowly shifted toward debates about formal immanence, emergence, the diagram, and issues surrounding the biological body. And in the Anyone Corporation's *Writing Architecture Series*, John Rajchman and Elizabeth Grosz leaned heavily on Deleuze to probe a number of acknowledged concepts of architecture—such as "construction" and "space."[18] In 1994 then, R.E. Somol guest edited a double issue of *ANY* to reconsider the legacy of Rowe; many of the contributors challenged Rowe by calling attention to the theories of Bataille, on one hand, and Deleuze and Guattari, on the other.[19] These French thinkers' specific versions of base materialism largely detached the meaning of form from language, narration, history, and representation and based it on more direct, bodily, and emotional sensations produced by physical actions—such as rhythm, vibration, or spasm. As such, Lynn found in Bataille an apologist of the artistry of devious form and the devious body, which he deemed irreducible to ideal types and therefore inaccessible to Rowe. In this, the computer was described as an enabler of transformational processes, which were generative of a new universe of creative alternatives.[20] Stan Allen described Bataille's work as a more radical riposte to the challenges of the alleged ideology of *fin d'histoire*, which had attracted two opposite reactions in architecture: on one hand, there were those who thematized the exhaustion of the modern ideal of continual innovation and, on the other, those who reacted with a complete libertarianism and free play in the aftermath of the dissolution of all constraints. Rowe belonged to the former category, and he tended to proceed by objectifying the past. To go beyond the contemplation of history, Allen asked the question of how one might get out of Rowe's impasse of reflective inactivity by allowing a more immediate and promiscuous expression of liveliness and activism.

And Somol cast the "improper" artistic potential underlying Bataille's notions of *bassesse* and the *informe* against Rowe's insistence on the importance of the rhetorical face or facade of a building, which he had inherited from his interest in painting. One can claim that the two traditions of the neo-avant-garde and neoconservative postmodernism—each of which owe its dues to Rowe—parted over this question of faciality: while the latter hoped to preserve the face of architecture throughout the storms of passing time, the former dispensed with the model of frontality and faciality altogether. As such, Jim Stirling introduced oblique and leaning facades that Rowe found unreadable because they negated the frontal exchange between subject and object; Eisenman eschewed the rhetoric of the facade with the intention to undo the classical metaphysics of presence; and John Hejduk hyper-individualized the facade to the point where nothing in them seemed generalizable any longer. Finally, Kwinter ranked Rowe's views as part of classical reductionist theories of form, in which he identified the shared shortcomings that "they are unable to account for the emergence, or genesis, of forms without recourse to metaphysical models."[21] What these theories share is their inability to transcend the analysis of historical objects and, instead, engage the processes of formation themselves.

Deleuzianism had no doubt reinvigorated the discussion about architectural form throughout the 1990s, and its materialist philosophy of becoming helped to shift that interest away from representational form toward the notions of performative or active formation—toward what Deleuze called "possibilities of fact" in the context of his study of Bacon.[22] While the frequency of references to Deleuze in architectural writing started to decrease in the beginning of the millennium, the early aughts became the time for a new empirical basis for the discipline with the rise of the pro-practice movement in architecture, as well as so-called design-based research—both of which sought to reconnect architectural and design intelligence to the contemporary material and social contexts. As such, Koolhaas published the outcomes of his research studios, the *Harvard Project on the City*, which had taken its inspiration from an earlier episode of experimentation with design-oriented research—Robert Venturi and Denise Scott Brown's Las Vegas studio at Yale in the late 1960s. The premise of design research is that architecture starts with the empirical collection of data, where the "exacerbated differentiation" of the real is used to creatively eclipse all preconceived models of architecture. In this context, architectural form took on a different meaning.

In 2000, Columbia University's Temple Hoyne Buell Center for the Study of American Architecture hosted the symposium "Things in the Making: Contemporary Architecture and the Pragmatist Imagination"; the event was staged as a sort of vengeance of philosophy against the architects who had hijacked philosophy to manufacture their own culture of "criticality," which was increasingly perceived as overly complicated and therefore stifling by the younger generation. The conference title was taken from William James and evidences the desire of the conference organizers to reanimate architecture with a body of thought that valued the vitality and experimental creativity of action and the real over the passivity of contemplation and reflection; James claimed that "[w]hat really exists is not things but things in the making. Once made, they are dead, and an infinite number of alternative conceptual decompositions can be used in defining them."[23] The appropriation of William James's critique of intellectualism and abstractionism were a direct strike against Rowe's legacy in architecture.

In the few years following this conference, Somol, Sarah Whiting, and Michael Speaks made the case for a culture of the "projective" in architecture.[24] Each one of them was not only trained in the Roweian paradigm, but each also explicitly formulated his or her ideas in dialectic relationship to Rowe. In this context, Speaks claimed in 2000 that "today we stand at the end of an historical period of experimentation dominated by Rowe's little story."[25] The "little story" referred to Rowe's interpretation that when modern architecture was imported from Europe to the United States, its forms were separated from its socialist ideology—that in fact, Rowe removed the zeitgeist argument from modern aesthetics and suspended its formal innovations in an ahistorical (and static) space called the "discipline of architecture." For Speaks, architectural theory was subject to a similar fate, where European (mostly French) theory became the ubiquitous tool of the intellectual in American academia. "Rowe's little story," Speaks continues, "is equally applicable to 'theory,' . . . Theory, like modern architecture, was detached from its Continental origins and replanted in the States, where it took on a lighter, more occasional existence. Theory carried all the punch of philosophy without the windy German preambles and recondite French qualifications, without, that is, years of study, political affiliation, or deep knowledge." He concludes that "resolutely critical and resistant to an emergent commercial reality driven by the forces of globalization, weighed down by its historical attachment to philosophy, and unable to recognize itself as a new mode of commodified thought, theory has not been free or quick enough to deal with the blur of e-commerce and open systems. Ultimately, theory, and the avantgarde project it enabled, has proven inadequate to the vicissitudes of the contemporary world."[26] Theory and form are largely exchangeable in this statement and are considered to have brought architecture to a creative standstill. In defense of theory, Michael Hays and Alicia Kennedy attributed Speaks's attack on theory as "a new technocratic positivism of an architectural-managerial class is fusing with an older but ongoing experiential nominalism (an atomized, appetitive immediacy of experience), with the result that the larger abstract ambitions and the sweaty efforts of an older theory are being taken to task." At the same time, they affirmed that "the various lines of flight out of theory (the technomanagerial, the postcritical, the neopragmatist, etc.) are still products of theory's success (and, perhaps, excess)."[27]

The architectural debates in the early 2000s amounted to a reaction against the then dominant trends of theory, to which Rowe's intellectual legacy belongs, and possibly precipitated by Rowe's death on November 5, 1999. Architecture in this moment in time found new missions in the empiricism of fabrication, in the exploration of affective experiences and sensations, in questions of ecological and economical sustainability, in new social and political agendas, as well as in the instrumentalism of informational and digital technologies.

Technological Formalism

The second set of developments in the discussions of formalism after Rowe is determined by the advances of computer-aided design—especially since the last decade of the millennium—as they have revolutionized the methods of form generation and, furthermore, the culture of interpretation in architecture. Modeling and animation software, as well as algorithmic and parametric form-generating programs, have become ever more accessible to architects in both academic institutions and in professional practice. There are those architects who argue that this technology has brought about a new style of parametricism for a post-Fordist society and that the visual hallmark of this new architecture is seamless formal fluidity on all scales—from interior design to architecture and to urban design.[28] The question of a "new" style became, yet again, a central topic of architectural discourse in the context of the consecutive software that architects have been using—such as ALIAS, Form Z, MAYA, 3D Max, Rhino, Catia, Processing, Grashopper, and a few more. Arguments about the autopoetic capacity of digital design tools have emerged from the same affective turn of the humanities mentioned earlier, which built on "a dynamism immanent to bodily matter and matter generally—matter's capacity for self-organization."[29] With the rapidly evolving digital technologies of form generation in architecture, Rowe's theories seem to no longer provide much of a mechanism to recognize the inherent logic of form per se; his once energizing ability to read and compare antecedents across historical time seemed to recycle the same precedents and arguments and appears to have run dry in comparison to the morphological potential emerging from digital culture.

Rowe never made any explicit claims about the repercussions of digital technology as a ubiquitous design tool for architects—even in the 1990s, by which time it had become more than manifest that the digital and electronic media were going to have a consequential presence in architecture. However, he did make evident, more generally, his stance vis-à-vis the technological worldview in his disagreements with Reyner Banham. The author of *New Brutalism* and *Theory and Design in the First Machine Age* dismissed Rowe as a representative of "the most in-group of all groupy people . . . of a secret-type cult"[30] and as old establishment against the rise of a younger generation of architects in postwar Britain with a new ethics and orientation toward a technological future. Banham's own background in engineering determined his understanding of the relation between technological performance and cultural form, which made him denounce Rowe's aestheticist claims that forms can exist independent of the meanings, which their inventors gave them.[31] In reverse, Rowe felt that Banham had reiterated the redemptive dream of architecture of the 1910s and 1920s, according to which theory and practice could be made to perfectly coincide. Because this concurrence neither happened in the futurist 1920s, nor in the postwar age of consumer electronics, Rowe claimed, Banham's history of modern architecture simply turned into a record of disappointment: performance fell behind the promises of inexpensiveness, happiness, liberation, and, more generally, of the social revolution.[32] Against the progressivist fiction of the self-organizing technological world, from Archigram to Buckminster Fuller, which is now revived in the discussion about parametrical self-organization, Rowe saw architecture as an authored, interpretive, and historically conditioned cultural act.

No doubt, the rise of digital culture in architecture has turned the discipline away from its obsession with the semiosis of historical meaning; today's formal avant-garde appears to eschew all historical content and instead, sees architecture as the edited instantiation of the inner structural logic of algorithms—often "fed" with the information of Big Data. At the same time, architecture finds itself in a moment in time when the experimentation with complex digital form begins to lose the lure of its initial naiveté, and calls for conceptual integration into the disciplinary discussion. A more discerning understanding of history makes clear that the notion of historical precedent cannot simply be eliminated from the lexicon of architecture with the hope that in its wake, a space would open up for the genuinely new and unprecedented. And this is where Rowe can suddenly be made very relevant again; however, whereas his legacy is partly to be found in the analytical and discursive relationship between the architecture of the present time with its history of precedents, the notion of precedent has come to mean something different today than it did for Rowe.

The question is to determine which types of disciplinary analogies with the past can be transposed into the contemporary, digital culture in architecture so that its new designs can become "thinkable"—both formally and historically? Such a hypothesis can lean on a useful distinction Rowe had put forward in his and Robert Slutzky's "Transparency" essays—the differentiation between the literal and the phenomenal in architecture. Although obviously an argument about formal analysis in architecture, the theory is grounded in the study of specific historical precedents without any quotation of past architectural motives. Particular aspects of cubist painting and Le Corbusier's architecture are being mobilized to create a mode of analysis in architecture, which led away from early and mid-century modernism, and which established a very useful disciplinary discussion that hinged on the comparative study of architectures throughout historical time.

If one believes Rowe, architecture is invested in always finding new analogies with precedents and rendering them operative for the discipline. Rowe had implicitly hoped that his analytic formalism could weather the advent of a new technological and cultural episteme, and so while his invocation of precedent is still a useful model today, the analogies between past and present architectures have to be reconceptualized.

Rowe and Slutzky presented Le Corbusier's League of Nations project from 1927 as the epitome of a space built on phenomenal transparency, and contrasted the building's assertive planes—which are "like knives for the appropriate slicing of space"—to the "amorphic outline" of Walter Gropius's Bauhaus.[33] Theirs was an argument about the analytical and geometrical rigor of Corbu's building complex—conceptualized as a series of spatial elements inserted in a matrix of parallel striations. By abstracting one spatial dimension ("deep space") into a simple stratification, they made it possible to compare the forms of the various sliced planes, and register their formal similarities and differences. This method of analysis was two-and-a-half-dimensional in that the attributes of deep space were compacted into a series of flat, variating diagrams not unlike the compression of different viewpoint onto the flat canvas in cubist painting. Each one of the diagrams contained "intimations of depth" and could only be decoded in an active intellectual act. Deep space was thus not simply a physical attribute of a building, but the result of a psycho-philosophical reading of an ideal perceiver of architecture, whose visual literacy is built on the knowledge of historical precedents.

Although ostensibly conceptualizing a modern building of the 1920s, Rowe's analytical tool reflects the dialectic space conception that would lead to the postmodern in architecture: in particular, the oscillation between two incongruous formal states of deep space—phenomenal transparency being "an argument between a real and ideal space"[34]—is seen as the engine that produces formal complexity. For this intricate morphology to be readable then, it has to be disassembled into a series of discrete formal fragments. In general, postmodern architecture always derived its formal richness from the confrontation between the absolute and the contingent—between the ideality of intellectual form and the reality of actual form.

Today, however, the assumption that architectural form is decoded from the vantage point of an "ideal" observer in the dialectic between real and ideal diagrams, seems out of sync with the way architects conceive and think of spatial structures. With today's ubiquitous computer-aided design technology, it is highly questionable whether Le Corbusier's belief that the plan is the generator (which proved so central to Rowe's "flat" view of the "mathematics" of a building) can be upheld as a mantra. Today, all buildings have turned literally transparent as wireframes on computer screens, and so the generator is mostly volumetric to start with, and can be thought of, and represented as, a diaphanous and approximate sphere of relationships rather than a rigid (fragmentary) geometry. An example of such a volumetric diagram can be found in UN Studio's Möbius House, which builds on the twisted and involuted logic of two lines that contain volumes of space and intersect in specific points. This building cannot be analytically striated to yield information about "deep space" in terms of Rowe's linear and layered notions of transparency and mathematics; its rational diagram, which was first conceptualized in the 19th century by astrologist and mathematician August Ferdinand Möbius, loops in all directions of space rather than simply from the inside of the building toward its facade. Despite the Möbius House's partially literal transparency in terms of windows, no standpoint in space affords the "total" view of the diagram: it requires a volumetric reconstruction; the formal clues for such a mental construction are distributed through space rather than compressed into the flat surface of a facade.

In the "Transparency" text of 1963, Rowe and Slutzky preempted a critical difference, which would, in the 1990s, become a central theme of discussion in architecture—Deleuze's distinction between the smooth and the striated—when Rowe and Slutzky contrasted the stratified diagram of the League of Nations project to the "amorphic quality" of the Bauhaus. The Bauhaus was deemed much less complex and of a different architectural species than Le Corbusier's building, because all formal differences were incorporated into the continuum of synthetic form and thus rendered illegible to Rowe: "By contrast [to the League of Nations]," Rowe and Slutzky wrote, "the Bauhaus, insulated in a sea of amorphic outline, is like a reef gently washed by a placid tide."[35] The word choice of *amorphic* is telling because it was coined as a critical term just about a decade and a half before Rowe used it: in 1946, American geneticist Hermann J. Muller used it to denote the kind of genetic mutation that disrupts the translation of the genetic code; this is to say that the amorphic is a "genetic null" mutation that causes the loss of all genetic information from one generation to the next.[36] In Rowe's understanding, one can assume that the Möbius House is a "genetic null" mutation in that the code or mathematics of precedents becomes illegible within the particular history of precedents he had proposed.

However, we have reached a point in history at which a majority of architectural projects are based on morphological attributes, which would rank them in Rowe's category of the amorphic—including the Möbius House; this does not mean that architecture has disengaged from its history but that Rowe's model of precedent and formal analysis needs updating. To fill the conceptual void, architectural culture in the early 2000s switched to a type of discourse that foregrounded the search for a terminology of aesthetic effects, but this trend, too, is running out of steam because it is fundamentally aimed at producing a mere inventory of sensations without relation to the broader disciplinary context and history. The digital means of form genera-tion, analysis, and representation should make it possible to read in a different way in relation to precedents, and to therefore realize that the term *amorphic* is used by analysts of form when they are unable to explain the relation of that form to the system of historical analysis used.

Disciplinary History of the Volumetric

Rowe and Slutzky's formalist-historicist conglomerate of "phenomenal transpar-ency" is futile to analyze a whole branch of space conceptions, which have a new relevance today: from Francesco Borromini's San Carlo alle Quattro Fontane, to Dominikus Zimmermann's Church of Wies, to Erich Mendelsohn's Einstein Tower, to Frank Lloyd Wright's Guggenheim Museum, to Eero Saarinen's TWA terminal, and to Alvaro Siza's Iberê Camargo Foundation. Their diagrams are volumetric in the sense that they are irreducible to any two-and-a-half-dimensional spatiality and thus resist the logic of cubist montage on a flat surface with intimations of depth. But these bulging, winding, interweaving, looping, bending, flexing, twisting, and bowing morphologies, which have taken center stage in contemporary design, do not have to be deemed "unreadable," they need their own discourse of precedent to be constructed. This history of precedents has never been written—in fact, it has been off the table on grounds of their "expressionism," in which artistic license was argued to replace rational logic, and therefore all energy to conceptualize their for-mal order was seen as wasted. In the Rowean paradigm, the world was divided along the formalist lines of Hans Scharoun versus O. Mathias Ungers, or expressionism versus rationalism. This differentiation, however useful to Rowe's worldview, is now undermined by the ability of digital technology to rationalize spatial orders that are based on the formal complexities of both so-called expressionist and rationalist architecture.

Spatial form rests on a different epistemological basis today in comparison to three, four, or five decades ago. As such, Rowe's distinction between classical nine-square versus modern four-square grids, which he extracted from Palladio and Le Corbusier, can be replaced with a discussion about the relationship between volumetrically defined centripetal versus itinerant organizations—between structures that define a center and those that explicitly avoid a center: Coop Himmelb(l)au's BMW Welt is spatially centripetal, whereas Studio Fuksas's MyZeil Shopping Mall in Frankfurt is itinerant. While both elaborate on the kinetic theme of the swirl, Coop Himmelb(l)au emphasizes the horizontal ribboning of the glazing diagrid whereas Studio Fuksas stresses the diagonal, upward banding. The precedents for these buildings exist, but their analogy with current architecture needs to be retheorized: Ledoux's architecture is centripetal and respects the horizontal datum; Piranesi's tends to be itinerant as well as ascending; none of these qualities, however, can be analyzed in terms of flat diagrams—be they plans or bundles of "phenomenal" sections. Phenomenal transparency manifests itself in other ways in these examples than in the formal clues a "facade" has to offer—in a frontal, directed, flattened manifestation to a distant viewer who stands in a fixed position in the space outside of a building.

The space outside the building is the realm Rowe imagined his analytical viewer to occupy; he did this when he analyzed Le Corbusier's La Tourette and Villa Stein and Palladio's La Rotunda, among other projects. This is because Rowe's thinking was firmly rooted in the episteme of the "critical century," which held that the act of reading and analysis hinged on the possibility of stepping back and distancing the subject from the object of analysis like in an X-ray view. Here, the assumption was that a design was successful when the dialogue between center and surface of an object could happen without too much loss of information—when essence and expression could coincide in a transparent continuum.

Nevertheless, volumetric diagrams are mostly unreadable from their outsides; the spherical diagram of the Pantheon, for example, is fundamentally interiorized. Equally, Frederick Kiesler's Endless House can only unravel its itinerant logic from within the volumetric diagram. Jean Nouvel's Tokyo Opera House project is highly articulated in its interior but reveals those geometries through a mere bulge on the exterior volume of the building. Similarly, UN Studio's looping Galleria Centercity in Cheonan, South Korea, offers a diaphanous swelling of the volume on the outside, which corresponds to formal pressures from the inside of the building mass. These diagrams transition from a high-resolution spatial articulation in their centers to low resolution at their periphery. The local bulge of Nouvel's Opera House facade suggests the location of the bulky, squarish objects in the building's interior, whereas the elongated swell of UN Studio's Galleria insinuates the spatial trajectory of circulation flows throughout the building.

San Carlo is one of the precedents of this inside–outside logic, in which the high-definition geometry of the volumetric diagram inside the building transitions into a low-resolution bulge on the outside. It is as if Rowe's ideal standpoint for the analysis of the building had been inverted and is, in this instance, interiorized and situated within the architectural object. The idea of the gradual loss of information through transparent media from inside to outside was missed by Rowe and Slutzky because their paradigm of analysis was built on an epistemology and aesthetics of sharp ruptures rather than of a gradual transformation of information through space. This changed understanding of transparency seems to have something to do with the incorporation of the contemporary analytical viewer in the context of digital media: the new media of representation are always converging on the multiple, orbiting views of the avatar of virtual space.[37] This is not an argument for a phenomenological approach to analysis in the endoscopic sense of virtual walk-throughs and animations but for a different attitude toward the analytical construal of architectural form today.

If phenomenal transparency is going to remain a useful analytical category for architects, it needs to be recast with certain modifications: the analyst has to be thought of as internal to the volumetric diagram, and the environment has to be conceptually unraveled from the inside out rather than with parallel striations in abstract space. It also has to integrate the notion of gradual morphological transformation through space instead of presupposing a homogeneous Euclidean space: the progressive loss of transparency might better be captured in the expression of *phenomenal penetrability*. Rowe never explicitly thematized the gradual diminution of information throughout the transparent system of stratification. Yet unlike the concept of transparency in cubism, digital culture has brought back to the table a characteristic endemic to literal transparency in the physical world—the morphological transition from high to low resolution in the passage through a medium—for example, by offering ways to conceptualize the conversion of precise geometric articulation into mere bulging. The bulge indicates the thatness of a volumetric diagram over the whatness of it. The position of analytical readability, however, is only offered inside the building.

The decreasing usefulness of Rowe's analytic method in the context of the contemporary avant-garde denotes a changed understanding of space today. The hegemony of volumetric diagrams over striated ones in contemporary architecture calls for a new comparative history of precedents based on the analogies and morphological characteristics that are relevant today.

What seems unchanged, however, is Rowe's idea that the comparative and analytical confrontation of present and past architectures is one of the most potent—both critical and operative—ways to theorize architecture. And one can agree with Bernhard Hoesli when he claimed that what is so central to Rowe's thinking is that it "reminds us that architecture exists only in relation to a theory of architecture."[38] In other words, when Rowe studied Inigo Jones's drawings for his MA research at the Warburg Institute in London (1945–48) under Rudolf Wittkower, he speculated in fact that Jones had not simply envisioned a series of discrete architectural projects, but that, considered as a whole, these individual designs built up to a "theory" of architecture much like Palladio's or Scamozzi's.[39] This is no doubt a powerful idea, because it argues that architects are not simply service providers to diverse clients and stakeholders who seek isolated solutions but also that they act from the standpoint of a disciplinary and conceptual expertise, in which buildings, on one hand, and ideas, on the other, are always in dialogue.

Notes

1 Parts of the section "Technological Formalism"—was formerly published as "Spherical Penetrability: Literal and Phenomenal" in *Log* 31 (Spring/Summer 2014): 31–39.
2 Colin Rowe and Fred Koetter, *Collage City* (Cambridge, MA: MIT Press, 1978), 148.
3 The strip cartoon Rowe referred to is reprinted in Bill Watterson, *The Indispensable Calvin and Hobbes: A Calvin and Hobbes Treasury* (Kansas City, MO: Andrews McMeel, 1992), 248.
4 Colin Rowe, "History and Theory: Two Contradictory Categories?," June 26–27, 1997, video recording, gta archives, ETH Zurich: 119–40:1; 30:00 min into the recording.
5 Rowe, *As I Was Saying*, vol. 3, ed. Alexander Caragonne (Cambridge, MA: MIT Press, 1996), 2.
6 I noticed this when I reread Hoesli's "Addendum" to his translation of the "Transparency" essay into German: unlike Rowe, Hoesli still talks about transparency when manipulating building/urban *plans*, and almost never mentions collage. I speculate that, because Hoesli was not only an architect but also an artist who created many collages himself, for him, collage really had a different meaning than it had for Rowe.
7 After Ungers's tenure as the chairman at Cornell, Rowe paid a lot of attention to the drawings of one of Ungers's German students, Rainer Jagals; these drawings were not collages in the sense of the superposition and co-extensiveness of transparent forms, but they were well about the side-by-side coexistence of formally differentiated structures. They were in fact based on the more traditional technique of pictorial composition on an urban canvas.
8 Vincent Scully, *Earth, the Temple, and the Gods*, rev. ed. (New York: Praeger, 1969), 2–3; refer also to Robert D. Richardson, *Henry Thoreau: A Life of the Mind* (Berkeley: University of California Press, 1986), 265.
9 Redaktionarchplus and Erika Mühlthaler, eds., "Learning from OMU," *Arch+* 181/182 (2006): 182. For contemporary discussions of the Green Archipelago project, see Pier Vittorio Aureli, *The Possibility of an Absolute Architecture* (Cambridge, MA: MIT Press, 2011); Lara Schrijver, "OMA as Tribute to OMU: Exploring Resonances in the Work of Koolhaas and Ungers," *The Journal of Architecture* 13, no. 3 (June 2008): 235–61; and *The City in the City: Berlin, A Green Archipelago / a Manifesto* (1977) by Oswald Matthias Ungers and Rem Koolhaas with Peter Riemann, Hans Kollhoff, and Arthur Ovaska, a critical edition by Florian Hertweck and Sébastien Marot; UAA Ungers Archives for Architectural Research (Zürich: Lars Müller, 2013).
10 Rem Koolhaas, "What Ever Happened to Urbanism?" (1994), in *S,M,L,XL* (New York: The Monicelli Press, 1995), 959–71.
11 I borrow the term *horizontalism* from Stephen Graham, Lucy Hewitt, "Getting off the Ground: On the Politics of Urban Verticality," *Progress in Human Geography*, published electronically April 25, 2012, accessed June 10, 2012, http://phg.sagepub.com/content/early/2012/04/25.

12 Peter Sloterdijk, *Sphären III—Schäume* (Frankfurt am Main: Suhrkamp, 2004), 605.

13 Hal Foster, Rosalind Krauss, Silvia Kolbowski, Miwon Kwon, and Benjamin Buchloh, "The Politics of the Signifier: A Conversation on the Whitney Biennial," *October* 66 (Autumn 1993): 3–27, accessed June 10, 2014, http://www.jstor.org/stable/778752; and Hal Foster, Benjamin Buchloh, Rosalind Krauss, Yve-Alain Bois, Denis Hollier, and Helen Molesworth, "The Politics of the Signifier II: A Conversation on the "Informe" and the Abject," *October* 67 (Winter 1994): 3–21, accessed June 10, 2014, http://www.jstor.org/stable/778965.

14 See also Sanford Kwinter and Umberto Boccioni, "Landscapes of Change: Boccioni's "'Stati d'animo' as a General Theory of Models," *Assemblage* no. 19 (December 1992): 50–65; accessed June 10, 2014, http://www.jstor.org/stable/3171176: "Yet futurism's profoundest gift to our century was its seemingly hubristic attempt to link the biosphere and the mechanosphere within a single dynamical system."

15 Gilles Deleuze, *Francis Bacon: The Logic of Sensation* (New York: Portmanteau, 1992), 65.

16 Ibid., 100.

17 K. Michael Hays and Alicia Kennedy, "After All, or the End of "The End of," *Assemblage* no. 41 (April 2000): 6–7, accessed May 20, 2014, http://www.jstor.org/stable/3171267.

18 John Rajchman, *Constructions* (Cambridge, MA: MIT Press, 1998); and Elizabeth Grosz, *Architecture from the Outside: Essays on Virtual and Real Space* (Cambridge, MA: MIT Press, 2001).

19 "Form Work: Colin Rowe," ed. R.E. Somol, *ANY* 7/8 (September 1994).

20 I am mostly referring to Greg Lynn's ideas in "New Variations on the Rowe Complex," *Folds, Bodies & Blobs: Collected Essays* (Brussels: La lettre volée, 1998), 208. Lynn championed Rowe's idealist theory of architectural order by showing that the insistence on an underlying ideal and static mathematics of architecture, which is focused on recognizable or "eidetic" form (that is, marked by extraordinarily accurate and vivid recall especially of visual images), will iteratively cancel out formal multiplicity and differentiation in architecture. The increasing calculating power of computers and their capacity to quickly decompose irregular and intricate forms into a set of regular geometrical substructures, iteratively produces generations of form that tend toward always greater geometric abstraction and regularity. To oppose the "reductionist project" based on Rowe's idealist mathematics, Lynn looked for inspiration in the diversity of hive, swarm, and crowd behavior, which paradoxically combined maximization with randomness as basis for an alternative and less predictable mathematics of form.

21 Sanford Kwinter, "What Is the Status of Work on Form Today?," *ANY* 7/8 (1994):65.

22 Deleuze, *Francis Bacon . . .*, 65.

23 William James, *A Pluralistic Universe*, 1909, as quoted in *Pragmatist Imagination: Thinking About Things in the Making*, ed. Joan Ockman (New York: Princeton Architectural Press, 2000), 27.

24 R.E. Somol and Sarah Whiting, "Notes around the Doppler Effect and Other Moods of Modernism." *Perspecta* 33 (2002): 72–77.

25 Michael Speaks, "Which Way Avant-Garde?" *Assemblage* no. 41 (April 2000): 78, accessed December 15, 2013, http://www.jstor.org/stable/3171338.

26 Ibid.

27 Hays and Kennedy, "After all . . .": 6.

28 Refer, for example, to Patrik Schumacher, "Parametric Diagrammes," in *Diagrams of Architecture, AD Reader*, ed. Mark Garcia (London: Wiley & Sons, 2010). See also Schumacher, "A New Global Style" (2009), in *The Digital Turn in Architecture 1992–2012*, ed. Mario Carpo (London: Wiley & Sons, 2013), 241–57.

29 See Patricia T. Clough, "The Affective Turn; Political Economy, Biomedia, and Bodies," *Affect Theory Reader*, ed. Melissa Gregg and Gregory J. Seigworth (Durham, NC: Duke University Press, 2010).

30 Reyner Banham in *New Society*, March 17, 1966, reviewing Douglas Stephen, Kenneth Frampton, and Michael Carapetian, *British Buildings, 1960–1964* (London: Black, 1965); quoted in "Editor's Note" to *As I Was Saying*, vol. 1, ed. Alexander Caragonne (Cambridge, MA: MIT Press, 1996), ix–x.

31 In a lecture at Sci-Arc, Reyner Banham claimed, "You show someone a building with plain white surfaces stood up on stilts with strip windows around it, and people will, even now, understand that building to make certain promises. . . . That kind of mythology of forms is part of a language with which we think in the 20th century in the developed Western countries. We know that those shapes belong to those promises. . . . Adopting an ironical stance toward the architecture of the 1920s, which is the New York Five ploy, doesn't get you anywhere at all . . . and it leaves you always in a morally exposed position: you are using a language which once had certain important meanings . . . you can wax ironical over it—in the way Peter Eisenman or Colin Rowe does [but the initial meaning] won't quite go away." Sci-Arc Media Archive, 26 March 1976; 6:00–7:00 min into the video recording, accessed March 10, 2014, http://sma.sciarc.edu/subclip/reyner-banham-myths-meanings-and-forms-of-twentieth-century-architecture-part-two-clip_7772.

32 Rowe, "Waiting for Utopia," *As I Was Saying*, vol. 1, 78.

33 Rowe and Robert Slutzky, "Transparency: Literal and Phenomenal," *Perspecta*, 8 (1963): 45–54, accessed October 14, 2013, http://www.jstor.org/stable/1566901.

34 Ibid.

35 Ibid., 54.

36 H.J. Muller, "Further Studies on the Nature and Causes of Gene Mutations," *Proceedings of the 6th International Congress of Genetics* (1932): 213–55.

37 On the topic of the centrality of the subject in the digital era, refer to Ralitza Petit, "Avatar-Space: The Ego Inc.," *Perspecta* 44 (2011): 92–101.

38 Bernhard Hoesli, "Commentary," in Colin Rowe and Robert Slutzky, *Transparency* (Basel: Birkhäuser Verlag, 1997), 59, my emphasis.

39 Refer to Anthony Vidler, *Histories of the Immediate Present: Inventing Architectural Modernism* (Cambridge, MA: MIT Press, 2008), 64.

Mannerism

"This became a major point of difference between Rowe and myself. . . . I became a student of *Semiology*, prefigured by the American philosopher C.S. Peirce as *Semiotics*. . . . Rowe, who spent a lot of time in Italy, admitted to being thoroughly *Italianizatto*. He characterized me as being *Frenchified*."

MANNERISM AND MODERNISM

The Importance of Irony

Robert Maxwell

Mannerism was not even visible to art critics until early in the twentieth century. Max Dvořák included a full discussion of mannerism in his classes at the University of Vienna between 1918 and 1921, but it only became visible in Britain with the publication of *Mannerism* by John Shearman in 1967. I myself first became excited by the topic with the publication of *Manieristi Toscani* in 1944, which I acquired in 1948.[1] I couldn't read Italian, but the pictures spoke for themselves. In artists such as Pontormo, Bronzino we find excessive feeling combined with stylistic exaggeration. I was riveted; it even affected my own work: my thesis design combined a stylized front with a prosaic back. Colin Rowe was ahead of his time when he published his essay "Mannerism and Modern Architecture" in the *Architectural Review* in 1950, thereby bringing Mannerism to Britain. He had a lot of influence on my generation of architects, but his influence on James Stirling was decisive: Rowe persuaded him that Mannerism is crucial to our age, so that Stirling from the beginning of his career had already decided to become a modern Mannerist.

In his speech "Architectural Aims and Influences," his response to the award of the Royal Institute of British Architects (RIBA) Royal Gold Medal, Stirling acknowledges his interest while still a student in the "just arrived" modern movement, *the foreign version as taught by Colin Rowe*.[2] Rowe taught history of architecture, not so much as an academic discipline but because certain architects had made architecture enjoyable. He enjoyed Palladio, and Serlio, Scamozzi, Romano, Hawksmoor, Ledoux, Soane, Cockerell, Lutyens—all architects with an enlarged self-consciousness about their art. The common factor in all these preferences was a tendency toward Mannerist doubt, and it seems that some principle of contradiction that Stirling absorbed from Rowe joined with his own origins as a northerner who enjoyed teasing the English and gave him a *modus vivendi* for his entire career.

FIGURE 1   Stirling & Wilford, Staatsgalerie, Stuttgart (1977–84)

Credit: © Richard Bryant; Courtesy ARCAID (Stirling 47-890-1)

This would explain a tendency in Stirling toward order, linked to a tendency to break the rules, a simultaneous enjoyment of contradictory aspects. The idea of balancing opposing tendencies suggests something like a game. Stirling appears to have taken to heart certain effects in Mannerist architecture, where rules are followed in one part only to be broken in another. In his essay "Ronchamp and the Crisis of Rationalism" (published in the *Architectural Review* in March 1956) he says,

> The desire to deride the schematic basis of modern architecture and the ability
> to turn a design upside down and make it architecture are symptomatic of a

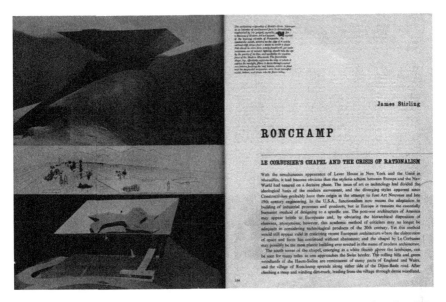

FIGURE 2 *Architectural Review*, page spread, March 1956: "Le Corbusier's Chapel and the Crisis of Rationalism" (Ronchamp, France), by James Stirling

Credit: Courtesy of Architectural Review, London

state where the vocabulary is not being extended, and a parallel can be drawn with the Mannerist period of the Renaissance. Certainly, the forms which have developed from the rationale and the initial ideology of the modern move-ment are being mannerized and changed into a conscious imperfectionism.

Rowe's essay of 1950, "Mannerism and Modern Architecture," was published just six years earlier, before Stirling had qualified as an architect. In it Rowe argues that architecture has twice become a theater for the expression of conflict: once in the Seicento, when Michelangelo showed the way into a post-Renaissance condition of anxiety, and again in the early twentieth century, when Le Corbusier found himself torn between the rational *tabula rasa* and his instinctive belief in evolution, by which things reached their perfect form by a step-by-step adaptation to the conditions of use. Evidently, the inherent contradiction between these two attitudes could have been a source of Mannerist doubt in Le Corbusier. Charles Jencks, in his book on Le Corbusier, makes it clear that he was torn in two by them.[3] The main charac-teristic of Mannerist art was to express the conflict between the current system and the promptings of disbelief and skepticism. The art both conforms to the prevailing system and subverts it at the same time. At the Palazzo Tè the voussoirs are correct, but seem to be slipping out. The emotion conveyed is one of discomfort, in which the beauty of the ideal is simultaneously asserted and questioned.

Rowe makes a good case for finding analogous qualities in the architecture of the 1920s, when there was a conflict between the abstract system of cubist composi-tion, where the personal vision of the artist is privileged, and the inherited system of neoclassicism still evident in works of Peter Behrens, early Walter Gropius, Adolf Loos, Art Deco cinemas and neoclassical American post offices. Where he had to search carefully to find contradictions between modernism as technicity and modernism as art, for us in the post-9/11 world, with global warming, after Darwin has shown the true age of the universe, after cosmologists have had to invent new concepts such as dark energy and dark matter to explain what they can't observe, the conditions in which we live supply all too readily the ontological grounds for doubt and uncertainty. Mannerism, instead of being a system for the periodization of art history, now becomes a condition in the production of art. We have finally reached what W.H. Auden called "the age of anxiety."

I met Rowe in 1940 soon after I entered the Architecture School at Liverpool University. He was the leader of a band of sophomores that used to come around the studios looking for fresh interest. I had become visible through a sketch design with the title: *The Last Day on which Milk Was Hand-delivered to the Housewives of Britain*; it showed a number of Corbusian villas on stilts, with ship's steps reaching to the ground, and a pair of milk bottles at the foot of each one. Rowe decided that I was interesting: he took me up. From then on, his thinking became my thinking. He led me to Le Corbusier, to Jacques Maritan, to Cyril Connolly. He introduced me to Sam Stevens, who taught us all to enjoy late Beethoven quartets. He introduced me to Douglas Stephen, whose partner I became, and to Rudolf Wittkower, who became the "client" for my design thesis.

Rowe sounded absolutely English, yet he made his career in the United States, where he taught at Cornell. But he began at the University of Texas at Austin, where, in only five terms, he changed architectural education for a generation of students on both sides of the Atlantic. He promoted buildings as people, with fronts and backs. Students began saying things like "my building addresses the park."

The insistence on seeing architecture at the intersection of thought and feeling gave his subsequent criticism an indubitably personal note, not unlike the art criticism of Adrian Stokes. Yet, without any public relations, without ever seeming to manage his career, he conveyed possibilities that have changed the course of architecture in both Britain and America. The finesse that he employed in introducing Corbusier and Mies to the school at Austin, Texas, was not so much premeditated as was precipitated by his intense sense of personal relations.[4]

This acute sense of the social gave Rowe's view of architecture an important freedom from standard art-historical classification. By the same token, architecture of any period could be scrutinized for its potential today. It is indirectly due to Rowe that many students studying for the doctorate at Princeton, and at other places, are architects by training, and approach the historical evidence with an understanding of how buildings come about. Thus, without caring a fig for Cultural Studies, he brought Architecture squarely into culture. That is, he brought architecture into the conversation, and since he had read widely, his conversation was erudite, and architecture fell into its natural place there as Mistress of the Arts. He made it clear that it could be used to express ideas, and was therefore an important contributor to the life of ideas.

Colin spoke always with a touch of irony, with complete knowingness. His awareness was total, yet his feelings were real, never affected. His words were persuasive, because he always addressed you directly, privately. This quality, translated to his written texts, allowed him to make insinuations that were compulsive, without ever asserting conclusions that went beyond the evidence he considered. No wonder he influenced so dramatically the teaching of architecture in the United States, by linking design studio to history and theory.

Rowe was one of only three scholars awarded the Gold Medal of RIBA during the twentieth century, the others being Nikolaus Pevsner and Sir John Summerson. If the RIBA recognized Rowe's achievement, it was not through popular acclaim but because through a process of selecting nominees for the Gold Medal that has remained at the discretion of the president and open to informed opinion. And there existed a body of informed opinion, led by Edward Jones, which saw him as a truly exceptional figure, one that influenced the course of twentieth-century architecture not by building but by inspiring others with an idea of architecture, and among those, above all, Stirling.

Rowe had the erudition of a scholar, but the taste of an aristocratic amateur. He enjoyed architecture as a form of theater, and he sent his students to the library not so much to study, as to crib ideas for their designs. In Britain, Rowe's influence as a teacher was circumscribed, very probably through a general aversion to his taste for asserting the importance of feelings rather than facts. In Britain, facts were treated as parts of nature—not seen as existing within culture. In the United States, however, Rowe had an enormous influence on a generation, mainly through his teaching at Austin. The saga of Rowe's intervention in the studio has been documented in Alex Carragone's book *The Texas Rangers*.[5] In collaboration with the design teacher Bernhard Hoesli, he outlined an entirely new framework for teaching architectural design, introducing as models not only Frank Lloyd Wright but then Mies and finally "Corbu" as well. This created the legend of the *Texas Rangers*, a band of teachers who saw a way of teaching modern architecture consistent with traditional architectural principles; the Corbusian slant was to inform the achievements of the New York Five.

Rowe was not only a historian; he was a qualified architect. Like Summerson, he enjoyed modernism because it provided direct access to the perennial game of architecture, but he did not share Summerson's doubts about the importance of the program.[6] He was a formalist who valued form not as good form, that is, not as conformity, but as a precise means of articulating ideas.[7]

As his article on "The Mathematics of the Ideal Villa" makes clear, by drawing parallels between the proportional systems used by Palladio and Le Corbusier, Rowe enjoyed the continuity between modern architecture and its past. His interest was in formal schemata, whose influence might be thought to lie beneath the surface as a species of "deep structure" and could therefore be discovered in works of very different provenance.

When Rowe became a lecturer at Cambridge University, Peter Eisenman fell under his spell and was induced to study Giuseppe Terragni closely and to become interested in Italian Mannerism. For him contradiction opened the way to deconstruction. Rowe's teaching was also known outside the university, it reached a wide audience and created a general compulsion. When he became Professor of Architecture at Cornell University a whole generation of students learned about the social nature of city space, well before it became a new orthodoxy, the inspiration for *new urbanism*. His enthusiasm for the inherent contradictions to be found in Italian mannerism, allied to frequent trips to Italy, created something of a legend. When he inhabited a flat in the Palazzo Massimi, during a spell at Rome for Cornell University, it seemed perfectly appropriate, a personal apotheosis. His experience of Italian cities, where the still vital tradition of the *passagiatta* continued to represent the popular appeal of city space, gave him an acute sense of the space as social, and conferred on his ideas an important freedom from the traditional art-historical approach. His essay "Mannerism and Modern Architecture" was published in 1950 following his "The Mathematics of the Ideal Villa" in 1947.[8] Both opened a discussion of modern architecture's continuity with the past that had an effect on the development of post-modernism in the 1970s. However, the discussion of mannerism as such has remained embedded in an art-historical framework. Rowe expected a much wider discussion, particularly on the repercussions of mannerism within modern architecture. In his introductory note to the reprinting of this essay in his book of 1976, he says,

> Since the writing of this article the initiatives of Robert Venturi have, to some extent, illuminated the situation. Nevertheless, while Venturi has been quite unabashed in his parade of elements of Mannerist origin and while, by these means, he has extended the theater of architectural discourse, the theme modern architecture and Mannerism still awaits the extended and positive interpretation which it deserves.[9]

Venturi has been dubbed *the father of postmodernism*. This was basically because he blew open the myth of functionalism, abandoning the claim that everything he did was "caused" by a practical necessity. A great part of it was due to his own preferences, his own wishes, and his own taste intervened between the analysis of the problem and the final result. In other words, the result was in some sense personal and therefore arbitrary, not inevitable. In admitting the importance of his own preferences, he struck a blow for truth over illusion and, in the conditions pertaining under functionalist dogma, made a significant contribution to theory. His ideas about complexity and contradiction are shared with modern mannerism. Yet he considers himself simply a modern architect, and it is not clear how much he is interested in the problematics of form as such. Rowe, on the other hand, was really excited about ambiguity and its role in dealing with uncertainty.

In "The Mathematics of the Ideal Villa," Rowe had pointed to Le Corbusier as "in some ways, the most catholic and ingenious of eclectics"—a characterization which prized him loose from the grip of functional fanatics, creating a perspective that did eventually lead to postmodernism in architecture. This was to emphasize the part played by form in Le Corbusier's system. Form, I have suggested, is primary, but it takes on meaning only in the total context.

Postmodernism in architecture, came about explicitly only in the seventies, but its main characteristics were already present in the other arts from the beginning of the twentieth century. In literature, we find fragmentation, allusions, historical, and other references in abundance in James Joyce's *Ulysses* and in T.S. Eliot's *The Waste Land*. In painting, synthetic cubism is a mixture of fragments and references, structured by abstractionism: Picasso's *Demoiselles d'Avignon* were followed by neoclassical fat ladies. In music, Varèse began the process of breaking music down to a series of sounds and Erik Satie's version of "background music" was a mixture of stylistic fragments, but his *Gymnopedies* and *Gnossiens* have become popular tunes, ironically often heard as background music.

Modernism took a postmodern slant from its inception, and only in architecture did the quest for pragmatic determinism lead to the dominance of functionalism, where everything was due to use, and nothing was left to be a matter of choice. But it is only through the exercise of choice that any product can approach the status of art. Today, at last, we can see that architects are putting their work in a framework of ideas. And the framework of ideas, today, is more and more concerned with the human condition and the uncertainty in which it operates.

Rowe made a great impression on all his fellow architects by his promotion of the *blank panel*, initially presented in the early work of Le Corbusier at the Villa Schwob at La Chaux-de-Fonds. This house was left out of the *Oeuvre Complète*, and treated as a kind of forerunner rather than as part of the modern repertoire.

FIGURE 3   Le Corbusier, Villa Schwob, photograph of front facade with blank panel
Credit: © F.L.C. / ADAGP, Paris / Artists Rights Society (ARS), New York 2014

The plan is fairly classical, and the heavy brick cornices would seem to make it quite old-fashioned, but even from an old-fashioned point of view the blank panel at the center of the entrance side stands out as something bizarre and arresting. Rowe says,

> Contemplating this facade for any length of time, one is both ravished and immensely irritated. Its moldings are of an extreme finesse. They are lucid and complex. The slightly curved window reveals are of considerable suavity. They reiterate something of the rotund nature of the building behind and help to stress something of the flatness of the surface in which they are located. The contrast of wall below and above the canopy excites; the dogmatic change of color and texture refreshes; but the blank surface is both disturbance and delight; and it is the activity of emptiness which the observer is ultimately called upon to enjoy.
>
> Since this motif, which is so curiously reminiscent of a cinema screen, was presumably intended to shock, its success is complete.... By its conclusiveness, the whole building gains significance; but, by its emptiness it is, at the same time, the problem in terms of which the whole building is stated; and thus, as apparent outcome of its systematically opposite values, there issue a whole series of disturbances of which it is both origin and result.[10]

These disturbances, as here described by Rowe, are perfectly compatible with the kind of inherent contradiction and ambiguity that Venturi was later to exploit as mannerist, and to build into his theory of complexity and contradiction. He even adopted the slogan: *Mannerism, not Expressionism.*

But the phenomenon of a blank panel at the Villa Schwob is located in a twentieth-century example. Now it remained for Rowe to find an example from the age of historical mannerism. Naturally, he goes where he has already been, to Palladio. And so we have two examples from sixteenth-century Italy: Palladio's Casa Cogollo, Vicenza, and Federigo Zuccheri's project for a Casino in Florence. The latter was meant to show Zuccheri as a master of sculpture, painting, and architecture, and this "blank" panel was intended to receive a painting. But there was a difficulty in putting a painting into the space of the engraving, so his blank panel remains sufficiently blank to figure in Rowe's sequence. Rowe knew of no plans to fill the blank panels in Cogollo and in Villa Schwob, and they therefore seemed to be genuinely blank, to offer in a prime location at first-floor level a genuinely contradictory element.[11]

Howard Burns has shown that this entire argument is based on a fallacy: the blank panels at Casa Cogollo and again at the Villa Schwob were both intended by their architects to receive a painting. That is why they were left blank.[12] But, erroneous or not, the effect Rowe's theory made on fellow architects was enormous, and aroused a wide interest in mannerism. Indeed, I consider it a major influence on architects today. When a speaker from the floor recently suggested to Eric Parry that his design for the Holbourne Museum at Bath was mannerist, he was happy to agree. The decorated cornice on his recent building in Piccadilly is nothing if not mannerist.

FIGURE 4 Casa Cogollo, main facade, Vicenza; attributed to Andrea Palladio (1559) in Otta vio Bertotti Scamozzi, Il forestiere istruito delle cose più rare di architettara, Vicenza, 1791, tar. XXVI

Credit: Courtesy Centro Internazionale di Studi di Architettura Andrea Palladio, Vicenza

It is certainly extraordinary that the High Renaissance, as established in architecture by Bramante with his design for the Tempietto of S. Pietro in Montorio, of 1502–10, was of such short duration. Designs by Raphael and Michelangelo of around 1520 already show signs of mannerist complexity, so that if one dates its beginning in architecture from the design of Bramante's Tempietto, his first work in a mature style, it lasted less than twenty years.

Even if the High Renaissance in painting is considered to start with the maturity of Leonardo around 1480, as John Shearman suggests, it hardly lasted forty years.[13] The hundred years from 1520 to 1620 are the years of Mannerism. It's rather amazing that the period of classic perfection should be so brief, as if it depended on an exact balance of forces, and perhaps it did.

Michelangelo's cartoon for *The Battle of Cascina* (1504–5) already fixes one of the main characteristics: containing a scene of emotive power in an artificial framework. The fighting figures form a compact block, which is complete well before we come out to the physical frame. It is a point that demonstrates the contrast between emotive content and formal device. It emphasizes the *coolness* of the style and the special balance between form and content that it makes into a method.

Michelangelo almost invented the style single-handed, as we can see from examining his figures on the ceiling of the Sistine Chapel: incredibly emotive, but also stylish, which results in a special enjoyment of art as both excessive in manner and contained by form. He really did invent the blank panel: as you emerge from the Laurenziana Library, standing at the top of the stair, the central bay opposite you has no aedicule, as do the others. It is an empty bay. With the pilasters being recessed, it combines blankness with contradiction, and in this, at least, Rowe was essentially right.

In his essay on Mannerism, he then proceeds to discuss the architecture of the late nineteenth century, by which time the classical style had been replaced by an eclectic variety, with an opposition between two trends: structural idealism in a rationalist mode, and picturesque composition in a romantic and visual mode. This dialectic

FIGURE 5 *Battle of Cascina*, after Michelangelo by Bastiano da Sangallo (ca. 1542)

FIGURE 6   Michelangelo,Vestibule of Laurentian Library, Florence (1525–71)

Credit: © Massimo Listri, Florence

already contains the 1970s opposition between functionalism and pastiche. There may be here a more general dialectical system, but Rowe does not pronounce on this, and so far as the later developments of the art of hermeneutics or interpretation are concerned, and particularly the ideas of semiotic theory, he dismissed all that as a form of jargonese.

This became a major point of difference between Rowe and myself. I was entirely convinced by the arguments of Ferdinand de Saussure, Claude Lévi-Strauss, Roland Barthes, and Jacques Derrida. I became a student of *Semiology*, prefigured by the American philosopher C.S. Peirce as *Semiotics*.[14] My farewell lecture at the Architectural Association was titled "Hommage à Barthes." Rowe, who spent a lot of time in Italy, admitted to being thoroughly *Italianizatto*. He characterized me as being *Frenchified*.

In his book with Fred Koetter, *Collage City*, Rowe the formalist acknowledged the temporary condition of city form. So long as the city continued to grow it could never reach utopia, which exists nowhere. He accepted Karl Popper (*Conjectures and Refutations*) and saw that the city was an ongoing situation, with no certain outcome. That is why I characterized it as a triumph for common sense.[15]

Yet, there is, I suspect, a certain reluctance in Rowe's acceptance of Popper. With Hegel, he admitted to a certain fatigue. I have a feeling that Rowe was skeptical about all science and believed above all in the power of beauty. He preferred art to science. I myself, in my inaugural lecture on becoming a professor at the Bartlett, spoke of *the two theories of architecture* and emphasized the separation between them.[16]

Today, science takes over the "explanation" of the universe, and of our place in it. Yet, in that explanation, it does not even seek to explain the power of beauty, not only by the way in which sexual attractiveness creates new life, but as a thing-in-itself, unconnected to biology. And it has no explanation to offer for the universe itself. Billions of galaxies, each containing billions of stars! Certainly millions of planets capable of sustaining human life. Is the universe then a machine for creating life, and ultimately, thought? That certainly is beyond belief!

But in pushing mannerism as an aspect of modern architecture, Rowe was truly wise. This expression of the uncertainty of our times makes doubt an essential part of our shared framework. At least we must be aware of this doubt, which means designing with a certain irony. One is no longer in the best of all possible worlds, and may be descending into an increasingly grim future. The population growth of the world is accelerating, and with global warming, the climate is changing. To bring these factors into agreement, democracy may come to be abandoned. We are reluctant to look at these facts too closely.

Stirling, in work inspired by Rowe, anticipated the uncertain future by cultivating architectural jokes. In dangerous times, staying cool, using, and whistling in the dark. The importance of both men may soon come to be recognized.

Notes

1 Luisa Becherucci, *Manieristi Toscani* (Bergamo: Istituto Italiano d'Arte Grafiche, 1944).
2 "Architectural Aims and Influences" was published in the *RIBA Journal* in September 1980.
3 Charles Jencks, *Le Corbusier and the Continual Revolution in Architecture* (New York: Monacelli Press, 2000).
4 See Colin Rowe, "Texas and Mrs. Harris," in *As I Was Saying, Recollections and Miscellaneous Essays*, vol. 1 (Cambridge, MA: MIT Press, 1996), 25.
5 Alexander Caragonne, *The Texas Rangers: Notes from an Architectural Underground* (Cambridge, MA: MIT Press, 1995).
6 John Summerson, "Lecture at the RIBA: The Case for a Theory of Modern Architecture," June 1957.
7 This obviously depends on a certain regularity over a period, and it is true that today, with the work of Daniel Libeskind, Rem Koolhaas, and, above all, Zaha Hadid, form is to some extent escaping from functionality. But not entirely! We recently visited Hadid's new tower in Marseille, where expressive curves bring the high-rise down to earth, but leave its functionality intact. If it costs more, in order to be "artistic," that's a matter of choice for the client. It may bring him more into public notice. However, if we think about music, it becomes clear that there, form is primary, even if it has a broad connection to meaning. The long slow chords of *Ma Vlast* do indeed suggest the horizontal hills of a landscape but only because the title suggests it. The loose grip is emphasized by the way music is currently used to articulate feelings in films of all kinds, and especially on television, where it eventually disintegrates into a series of sounds, meaningless if heard on their own. But the use of background music in this way emphasizes the importance of form in the birth of

feelings. In all art, there seems to be an interest in pure chance, as a generator of interest. But chance is not necessarily interesting. Unless a succession of random sounds can be to some extent anticipated, the listener cannot be surprised when his anticipation turns out to be wrong, and it is that surprise that makes the interest. On this, see Abraham Moles, *Information Theory and Esthetic Perception*, trans. Joel E. Cohen (Chicago: University of Illinois Press, 1968).

8 Reprinted in Rowe, *The Mathematics of the Ideal Villa, and Other Essays* (Cambridge, MA: MIT Press, 1976).

9 Rowe, "Mannerism and Modern Architecture," in *Mathematics*, 29.

10 Ibid.

11 See also Rowe, "The Provocative Façade: Frontality and Contrapposto," in *As I Was Saying*, vol. II, 180.

12 Howard Burns in a symposium at the Royal Academy on *Palladio and his Influence*, March 2009, answering a question put by Robert Maxwell.

13 John K.G. Shearman, *Mannerism* (Harmondsworth, UK: Penguin, 1967).

14 C.S. Peirce, "Logic as Semiotic: The Theory of Signs," in *Philosophical Writings of Peirce*, ed. Justus Buchler (New York: Dover, 1955), 98–115.

15 See Maxwell, "Rowe's Urbanism in *Collage City*: A Triumph for Common Sense," in *L'architettura come testo e la figura di Colin Rowe*, ed. Mauro Marzo (Venice: Marsilio, 2010), 155.

16 Maxwell, "The Two Theories of Architecture," text of inaugural lecture in 1979, University College, London, 1982.

"But it was the confrontation of what Rowe later termed 'French studio language' and 'art historical language' that, as he remembered, provided the impetus, first for an experience of the United States, and then for the special blend of the two that characterized his mature criticism after 1947."

RECKONING WITH ART HISTORY

Colin Rowe's Critical Vision[1]

Anthony Vidler

> *You could say, I suppose, that with Labrouste everything is line and contour and profile and edge. You might even suggest that with Labrouste we are in the world of Ingres—very, very close to it. The ideal is intellectualistic, rationalist, near Renaissance, and, I suppose, in the end, Florentine.*
>
> *With Garnier, line and contour are obviously of very little significance. The Opéra is not so much sculpture as it is modeling, by comparison with the Library. It is not so much made out of iron—as the Library almost attempts to be, as made out of something like clay. And the prevailing idea is something like chiaroscuro, the overtones are physical and voluptuous, and near Baroque, and, I suppose, in the end, Venetian.*
>
> —Colin Rowe on Labrouste's Bibliothèque Sainte-
> Geneviève compared to Charles Garnier's Opéra,
> unpublished transcript of a lecture at the Institute for
> Architecture and Urban Studies, 1975

Neither a professional architect, although graduated from the most professional school in Britain at the time, nor an art historian, although trained by one of the foremost in the field, Colin Rowe was an exemplar of that hybridity characterized by his student and friend Robert Maxwell as "the architect-trained critic."[2] Indeed, he was emphatic in rejecting the idea that he was a historian, as when, reacting to a vindictive attack launched by a former admirer when presented with the Royal Institute of British Architects (RIBA) Gold Medal in 1995, he professed astonishment that the essay "The Mathematics of the Ideal Villa" could have even been conceived as "history" in the proper sense. He was, he explained, indulging in "an exercise in critical polemic, something entirely innocent of the least pre-pretentions to historical explication."[3]

Yet, on closer examination, this denial represented somewhat of a dissimulation, an avowal of his engagement in another kind of history, one that we might call loosely today, following Tafuri, "operative" history. And, as he was quick to point out, his MA advisor Rudolph Wittkower was equally open to the charge of advocacy in his Palladio studies, and as for Reyner Banham, who had been proposed as a more worthy medalist, he was never "the neutral dispassionate observer which the mythical 'historian' is supposed to be."[4]

Arguably Wittkower could reasonably be held to an art-historical standard, but Banham certainly shared an advocacy and often polemical-critical role with Rowe. Indeed both Rowe and Banham were among a remarkable group of British critics of their generation, most, like Robert Maxwell, trained as architects—Sam Stevens, Kenneth Frampton, Alan Colquhoun, and Robin Middleton, among others. As Tafuri recognized in setting them up as his principal intellectual adversaries, their influence on the writing of the history of the Modern Movement and on the practice of architecture itself was and has been profound.

The special character of Rowe's criticism, its own particular kind of hybridity—one that posed itself ex cathedra as if woven out of whole cloth and dependent on its author alone—has, however, always stood apart from the group. Rowe himself defended his originality against all comers implicitly and explicitly: implicitly by neglecting to footnote his sources, including, most prominently, his tutor Wittkower, and explicitly by his reluctance to indulge in autobiographical reminiscence.

This resistance to being characterized, pinned down as to method or school of thought, while reinforcing his self-imposed outlier status, and, as Banham complained, his status as "the only living British critic or architectural pundit to become not only the object of a secret-type cult, but also an anti-cult," nevertheless left him sidelined with a small group of admirers outside the mainstream of architectural history or theory.[5] Rowe as a phenomenon, as the "guru" of Ithaca, has been endlessly quoted, has inspired numerous students and architects, but, with certain notable exceptions, has escaped historiographical analysis. This fate would have pleased him immensely, but it reduces the contemporary importance of his published work, as scholarship seemingly undermines his premises, and critical theory adds him to the list of outdated formalists, out of Wölfflin and Hildebrand.

Rowe's defense against categorization, in fact, hides a complex web of intellectual sources that were seemingly seamlessly incorporated into his innate talent for visual recognition and memory to form a didactic stance whose rhetorical force from the outset gave the lie to its own evolution, its gradual emergence out of its Wittkowerian beginnings to its only apparent reification in the later stages of his career.

He left few clues—the brief introductions to his collected writings, a revealing association in a review or critique, a recalled incident or two. Liverpool between 1938–42 and 1944–45 provided the first intimations of the US—"at one time so conscious of its rapports with Savannah and Mobile and always conscious of New York."[6] The School of Architecture, founded with Charles Reilly's respect for McKim, Mead and White with a nod to the Paris Beaux-Arts' "exaltation of the plan," deepened the alliance. A gradual acceptance of the modern opened up by his successor Lionel Budden confirmed the school as "liberal and tolerant," a "late Beaux-Arts academy, ramshackle, vulgarly impressionist and deplorable in the Liverpool style, because of its patently vulnerable 'truths', its pretentious addiction to 'culture'," all added up to a congenial mixture for a Rowe already deeply distrustful of the "English" and "William Morrisy Architectural Association," with its "modern social consciousness" in a "Ruskinian version."[7]

FIGURE 7 Nicholas Hawksmoor, Proposition IV for Queen's College, street front, Oxford

Credit: Courtesy of The Provost and Fellows of the Queen's College, Oxford

FIGURE 8 Giuseppe Terragni, Novocomum Apartment Building, Como, Italy (1927–29)

Credit: © John Hill

His models and those of his contemporaries at Liverpool were the outliers to the tradition of British respectability—Hawksmoor, Vanbrugh, Soane, C.R. Cockerell—all those whose architecture did not, as Rowe reported Berenson remarking, "ooze prettiness." Join this to the presence of the Polish School in Exile, the first volumes of Le Corbusier's *Oeuvre complète*, and an already prescient interest in the work of Giuseppe Terragni, and the formation of a fundamentally academic, Beaux-Arts, vision of modernity that could encompass Leterouily and Sartoris, but not Ruskin or Marx, was complete.

Or almost so. For underlying this architectural acculturation was another, almost as powerful, that of Anglo-American literature and criticism, and again of the outlier kind. Here, Auden, himself between England and America, announcing an "age of anxiety" as if paralleling an increasing interest in Mannerism; and behind Auden, the anti-Ruskinians, Clive Bell, Roger Fry, and, for architecture, Geoffrey Scott and Adrian Stokes. With Warburg and Wittkower, in 1945 the German School entered the equation—Wittkower's own masters Wölfflin and Burckhardt—but also, and no doubt to the annoyance of the advisor, that more genteel version adopted by Pound, Scott, and Stokes, that surrounded Bernard Berenson at I Tatti. [8]

But it was the confrontation of what Rowe later termed "French studio language" and "art historical language" that, as he remembered, provided the impetus, first for an experience of the United States, and then for the special blend of the two that characterized his mature criticism after 1947. In personal terms, this conjuncture was stimulated on his first trip to Italy in that year, meeting the American art historian Craig Smyth in Florence, and on his second in 1950 encountering the San Franciscan Beaux-Arts architect Arthur Brown in Rome. The scene of the revelation was portentously enough, Carlo Rainaldi's Santa Maria in Campitelli; here Brown's architectural exposition of Rainaldi's use of light, the comparison with Vanbrugh, conflicted with the measured art-historical prose of Wittkower, whose article on Rainaldi had recently introduced Rowe to the analysis of Mannerism:

> The studio language, which belongs to the process of architectural education as it relates to the drawing board, is, of necessity, the voice of immediacy and enthusiasm. It is the voice of excited critics and intelligent students, who may, all of them, be largely ignorant. [. . .] But the art historical language is something other. It is the voice of caution and aspires to erudition; and if the studio language, always vivacious, is prone to be the language of uncriticized tradition, then the art historical language, often still attempting to realize that impossible ideal of Ranke's, simply to show how it really was will always operate to separate and divide. [9]

A sentiment only confirmed by Wittkower's reaction to the idea that the Beaux-Arts could ever have known, let alone understood, Rainaldi, launched Rowe's determination to explore the United States, where Henry Russell Hitchcock, against his former mentor's advice to go to Harvard and study with Sigfried Giedion, waited at Yale to replace Wittkower. From Hitchcock, Rowe gained an appreciation of Frank Lloyd Wright and an impulse to travel across the US, which led to the famous meeting with Mrs. Harwell Hamilton Harris in Norman, Oklahoma, whence came the equally celebrated invitation to join the faculty at the University of Texas, Austin.

All this, from Rowe's own scattered memoirs, and from what he gained in terms of historiographical/critical influences, are very much on the surface of his writings: a certain influence of Wittkower in "The Mathematics of the Ideal Villa" (the Palladian villa diagram) and on "Modern Architecture and Mannerism" (the essays on Michelangelo's Laurentian Library and Rainaldi); an enduring affinity with the "plan" from the attenuated Beaux-Arts diagrams of Guadet and Gromort; an ever-present enthusiasm of the studio, for experimentation and exploration, from that first encounter with Arthur Brown; and a certain distance from art-historical caution, exhibited in his critique of Pevsner's assumed "Englishness," Giedion's Hegelianism, fueled by Wittkower's methodological rigidity, which saw "The Mathematics of the Ideal Villa" as "deplorable and silly": "meretricious and a waste of time."[10]

It is, however, in the less acknowledged sources of his criticism that we can find substantive clues to his approach. His consistent mode of presentation, two slides side by side, compared and contrasted, immediately refers to the method pioneered by Heinrich Wöfflin, and one followed to the letter in the illustrations and text of "Mathematics." Indeed, this is one source admitted by Rowe, in his "Addendum" to the republication of the essay in 1973:

> A criticism which begins with approximate configurations and which then proceeds to identify differences, which seeks to establish how the same general motif can be transformed according to the logic (or the compulsion) of specific analytical (or stylistic) strategies, is presumably Wölfflinian [sic] in origin; and its limitations should be obvious.[11]

This admission was immediately qualified by his enunciation of the limitations of such a "Wölfflinian" method as unable "to deal with questions of iconography," as "over symmetrical" in its approach, and, if protracted in its close analysis, as likely to "impose enormous strain on both its consumer *and* producer." Nevertheless, in his new addendum to the republished essay he went on to propose yet another comparison of "approximate configurations," this time between those of Schinkel's Altes Museum and Le Corbusier's Palace of Assembly, Chandigarh, which he felt might lead to further comparisons with "certain productions of Mies van der Rohe." For, despite the faults of the comparative method, and its status as "painfully belonging to a period of c.1900," Rowe found that the merits of this "Wölfflinian [sic] style of critical exercise" lay in its primarily visual approach, "making the minimum of pretenses to erudition," the "least possible number of references outside itself," and thence its ultimate "accessibility." And in a characteristic expression of the mixture of irritation and boredom accompanying the arduous task of writing all this down, he added, "for those who are willing to accept the fatigue."[12] This combination of the Wölfflinian comparative method and accessible visual analysis was, of course, what led to Rowe's popularity among practicing architects and, conversely, his uncertain position in the guild of orthodox art historians.[13]

The outlines of the Wölfflinian method were well known and even seen as outmoded by the 1940s, but for Rowe they provided a ready matrix by which to contrast and compare and to set up pairs of characteristics, and thence pairs of objects, all measured according to the principle of side-by-side slide projection in the lecture room, a method pioneered by Wölfflin himself. It is probable that in referring to Wölfflin "c.1900" Rowe was thinking not of *Renaissance and Baroque* (1888), not translated until 1964, but of the later *Principles of Art History* (1915) with a first English translation in 1939, yet the general outlines of the approach were well known and must have been pervasive in the postwar teaching methods that Rowe must have experienced at the Warburg. His classic pairing of complementary opposites—linear/painterly, plane/recession, closed form/open form (tectonic/a-tectonic), multiplicity/unity, absolute clarity/relative clarity—appealed to those for whom the visual interpretation of a work was privileged over the iconographic or historical interpretation. Of these categories, perhaps the most important for Rowe was that of the development of plane to recession.[14]

In Wölfflin's schema, this was a process whereby the representation of pictorial space shifted from "the combination of forms in a plane as a principle," to a "definitely recessional type of composition," a move that took place between the 15th and the 16th centuries, between the period that Wölfflin called the "Classic" or High Renaissance and what he termed the Baroque. For Rowe's generation, this signified a shift between the High Renaissance and what was later understood as Mannerism, and Wölfflin's characterization is immediately recognizable as such: "in the former [Classic] case, the will to the plane, which orders the picture in strata parallel to the picture plane; in the latter ["Baroque"/Mannerist], the inclination to withdraw the plane from the eye, to discount it and make it inapparent, while the forward and backward relations are emphasized, and the spectator is compelled to co-relate in recession."[15] Following the celebrated comparison of Palladian and Corbusian villas, the chain of Wölfflinian style comparisons in Rowe's writing appeared endless: in "Mannerism and Modern Architecture," (1950) where the method was outlined in the context of specific formal gestures along the lines of Wölfflin's own "principles," and in "Neo-Classicism and Modern Architecture," (I and II, 1956–57), where the implications of "further comparisons with the productions of Mies van der Rohe" were fulfilled. In Wölfflin, Rowe found his urge toward dialectical thinking, at least diagrammatically, confirmed.

Yet, this affiliation, however long lasting, only provides a more or less structured outline of his approach: the content of these essays expands far beyond the narrow confines of comparison and contrast. Rather, the presentation of architecture gains its force from a decidedly individual technique of description, one approaching the "enthusiastic language" of the studio, but that is rigorously corrected by a combination of extraordinarily perceptive formal analysis and a more covert understanding of the psychology of vision, as well as a thorough absorption of its previous exponents.

Here we return to that alternative tradition of architectural explication that, in England was represented by Bell, Fry, Scott, and Stokes (themselves reacting against the equivalent tradition in the social-medieval terms championed by Ruskin), and that stemmed from an equally alternative approach to art history pioneered by Winckelmann: the "art" of the *description*.[16] In his celebrated descriptions, Winckelmann averred that he had "always looked at works of art with a certain enthusiasm," a description of what was seen demanded "the most sublime style," where the description of the work should evoke a parallel enthusiasm to that evoked by the work itself.[17] Revived as a counter to academic scholastics in the late 19th century by Walter Pater, Winckelmann's descriptions then passed into literary "restorations" of the classical world, as in Pater's own *Marius the Epicurean*. In Berenson's circle, Ezra Pound and Geoffrey Scott, followed by Adrian Stokes as Stephen Kite, have shown, invested the description of architectonics, with what Wölfflin understood as psychological empathy, and Pound as "patterned energy."[18] Rowe, while he rarely if ever speaks of this tradition in its British formulation, and who was attracted more to the Gestalt psychology of perception than to Stoke's Klienian analysis, was nevertheless deeply indebted to Stokes, even if, as generally the case, in opposition. *The Stones of Rimini* (1934), with its riveting descriptions of the Tempio Malatestiano; *Venice* (1944); *Art and Science* (1949); and *Smooth and Rough* (1951) were actively discussed at Cambridge in the years 1958–62, *Art and Science* being Sandy Wilson's favorite, and *Stones* and *Smooth and Rough*, Colin's.

But the movement toward enthusiastic description had begun earlier. While the MA thesis "The Theoretical Drawings of Inigo Jones: Their Sources and Scope" (University of London, November 1947) exhibits a fully formed ability of comparison (in this case between Jones and his model Palladio) intellectual and architectural, together with a method of façade close reading that predates his Mannerism essay by three years, intimations of a later descriptive force are restricted by the thesis's theoretical and philological subject-matter, its close readings of textual annotations and analyses of drawn exemplars. But in "Mathematics," Rowe's descriptive force is evident, set up by the compared "lyrical" descriptions by Palladio and Le Corbusier of the respective sites of Villa Capra and Maison Savoye. In fact the "mathematics" of the title is almost entirely subsumed within a dynamic formal and spatial analytical description of the villas under comparison: Malcontenta/Garches and Capra/Savoye.

This tour de force of reading is continued and surpassed in his analysis of the idea of Mannerism three years later. Here he goes beyond his named sources, Nikolaus Pevsner and Anthony Blunt, to develop the concept in elevation with respect to the facades of the so-called Casa di Palladio in Vicenza and Federico Zuccheri's Casino in Florence, and in plan with Michelangelo's Cappella Sforza and Vignola and Ammanati's Villa Giulia. These active and "studio language" descriptions are separated by a long excursus outlining the fate of the classical ideal from the Renaissance to Modernism—a critical historical essay that deserves more analysis than it has received—then to link the façade problem with the (supposedly) blank panel in Le Corbusier's Villa Schwob at Chaux-de-Fonds, and the plan problem to Mies van der Rohe's disaggregated plans for the Brick House project of 1923 and the Hubbe

House of 1935. And while this essay was completed at the height of the "Mannerist" moment identified by the Smithsons, Stirling, Maxwell, and Banham, its argument extends outside the commonplaces of purely stylistic effects linked to anxious social effects (culminating in Wylie Sypher's *Four Stages of Renaissance Style* in 1955) to provide a microcosmic reading of Le Corbusier's *Vers une architecture* considered in relation to his inherited classical tradition. In both "Mathematics" and "Mannerism," Rowe's ability to see material, tectonic moves in space and ornament as intellectually, philosophically, driven, lifts the argument into a realm that is fully constituted by the amalgam of studio and art historical language into the form of a eyewitness description—an activated eye often accompanied by a moving body that is almost cinematographic in its effect. This approach was to reach its finest exposition, however, in the analysis of the monastery of La Tourette, the last article he wrote before leaving Cambridge for Cornell in 1962, one of the very few of Rowe's articles to be devoted to a single building, with few comparative "Wölfflinian" examples to deploy.[19]

In December 1960 Colin Rowe stayed for three days in the Dominican monastery of La Tourette. The ostensible reason for the visit was to prepare a critical article for the publication of Le Corbusier's recently completed work for the *Architectural Review*. Returning to Cambridge for the Lent term, Rowe set about writing his piece, by all accounts, including his own, one of the more difficult he had attempted. The result was a long reflection, or meditation, on the potentials of a visual analytic that he had developed since 1947 for practical, experiential criticism. Significantly enough, he opened with a quotation from José Ortega y Gasset, an author whose newly translated works he had consumed with a passion, this one from *Meditations on Quixote*, Ortega's first book, from 1914, published in English for the first time only in 1961, as Rowe was writing. It was drawn from the Preliminary Meditation, the second section titled "Depth and Surface," and it encapsulated the perception that the later historians of Mannerism had exploited to the full: that "the dimension of depth, whether of space or time, whether visual or oral, always appears in one surface."[20] For Rowe, this sense of a flat surface expanding into depth through what Ortega terms the "foreshortening" that condenses two moments of vision into a single plane, the fusion of the "simple vision" of the material fact with the "purely intellectual vision" that constitutes the "second virtual life" of the surface, precisely summed up what he had been saying about Mannerism since 1950.

And indeed, the first sentence of the essay joins his first Corbusian conundrum—the blank panel at in the Villa Schwob at Chaux-de-Fonds—with his more recent experience of the north side of the church of La Tourette. The monastery is thus heralded as a potentially Mannerist in visual and virtual content with one cavil: that while both Chaux-de-Fonds and La Tourette present themselves at the first instance through these surfaces, motifs "without high intrinsic interest," once absorbed, cannot retain the eye's focus of attention.[21] But not without a second preliminary, also intellectual, visual exemplar. Here the focus is not on a surface with potential depth, but on the appearance of a building as a whole as approached by a visitor: that of the Acropolis as experienced by Le Corbusier: the landscape with the "false right angles"

FIGURE 9 Le Corbusier, Sainte Marie de La Tourette, Eveux, France (1956–60)
Credit: © Cemal Emden

of the composition, the "elements of the site" that "rise up like walls" powerful and cubic "like the walls of a room."[22]

This, all in order to initially deny the comparison to La Tourette, which is not a type of Parthenon, with a farmhouse that is not a Propylea, and is absent the Piraeus and Mount Pentelicus, which, in turn, is denied by similarities in the patterns of organization that reinforce the comparison: "compounding of frontal and three-quarter views," "impacting of axial directions," "tension between longitudinal and transverse movements," and, above all, the site—the "intersection of an architectonic by a topographical experience."[23] Once made, the unraveling of these deceptively simple comparisons takes up much of the rest of the essay.

At this point, however, Rowe drops what Ortega would call "purely intellectual" visual comparisons for three pages in order to introduce the monastery as encountered by a "casual visitor"—the experience of the direct and simple visual effect. The hill has been climbed (not an acropolis), an archway penetrated (not a propylea), and with a mansarded pavilion on the left and a kitchen garden on the right (two extremely everyday objects of the French provincial landscape), the visitor is confronted by a decisively unconventional phenomenon that is stripped of all pretense of an accommodating entry to a work of architecture: a "vertical surface gashed by horizontal slots," "an enigmatic plane" bearing "multiple scars" like the "injuries of time," with a series of three "gesticulating entrails" (to the initiated, *canons à lumière*) rising above its parapet. The visitor feels immediately "cold-shouldered" by the building.[24]

Of course, this particular visitor, who had instantly transformed his preliminary visual experience into an intellectual one, only now was able to name this *plane*, this *surface*, literally as the wall of the north side of the church. But here there appeared another ambiguity, for a frontally encountered "wall" is also evidently an elevation and generally a "front." However, at La Tourette, this elevation was not a front facade but a "flank," a "profile rather than a full face," noted Rowe, always one to equate facades and faces.[25]

The "visitor" is now plunged into an almost traumatic experience, "as unexpected as it is painful," indicating even "a presumable tragic insufficiency" in his status, without the "means of making coherent his own experience": "He is made the subject of diametric excitations; his consciousness is divided."[26] Such a condition is, as Rowe intends to intimate, akin to that attributed by Wölfflin, then Riegl, Schmarsow, Dvorak, and Pevsner, to the mannerist subject, which is compared so often in their writings to the anxious, alienated modern subject and then linked indissolubly to the expression of anxiety in forms that seem self-contradictory, juxtaposed discordantly, the "deliberate inversion" of classical or modernist rules, "[a] state of inhibition," as Rowe called it, "an attitude of dissent," an attitude that Le Corbusier shared, Rowe argued, with Palladio.[27]

Recovering himself, and comfortably reverting to his *intellectual* vision, the visitor, rather than simply turning around the corner to investigate the actual "front," instead then set out "to cross an imaginary picture plane" with the intent of discovering its frontal components, as if La Tourette might be ordered according to the rules of literal and phenomenal transparencies striating the League of Nations project. Here he was led not only one way by the oblique parapet and its false perspective but also the other way by the opening up of the steep vistas of the valley above which the monastery is set. At once the wall emerges as a pointer to "a space rifted and ploughed up into almost unbridgeable chasms." The hill might then just be an acropolis.

FIGURE 10   Le Corbusier, Sainte Marie de La Tourette, Eveux, France (1956–60)

Credit: © Miroslava Brooks

And the monastery a Parthenon? For despite all indications to the contrary based on previous experience, when the corner is turned "the anticipated frontal views" never materialize. The only front is a side: for the rest, all other views are foreshortened and presented at a three-quarter angle: "While other exposures, east and west, at the price of uncomfortable clambering around, may certainly be seen in frontal alignment, they are usually presented, and apparently intended to be seen, only in a rapid foreshortening."[28] Which point of view, Rowe argued, was similar to that presented by Le Corbusier/Choisy in the self-presentation of the Parthenon, a "modified three-quarter view." And, even as the blank panel of the Villa Schwob "generates a fluctuation of meaning and value" between positive and negative implications, so the north wall of La Tourette, with its false perspective, its twisting canons à lumière, sets up a double-spiral condition that is with some difficulty embedded in the flat surface of the plane itself, thus provoking a kind of visual "hallucination," an optical illusion that offers the key to the interpretation of the entire building.

In this way the understanding of the strange selection of the site is set up—its abrupt slope that seems perversely to counter the calm of a horizontal monastery type and the cubic cells that seem to counter the Dom-ino prototype, and this again countered by the "megaron" volume of the church—what Rowe refers to as "the crossfertilization of the megaron and sandwich concepts." It is this tension that leads Rowe back to his original Corbusian prototypes—Poissy, a sandwich; Maison Citrohan, a megaron; and to the conundrum of Garches that exploits the tension between the two, once again visually, through its two major facades that act as "planes which volatize the reading of depth."[29]

If, however, the shadow of Wölfflin, and by implication Riegl, is present throughout this imbricated reading, another intellectual father figure has emerged since the first essays on the ideal villa and Mannerism were composed: that of Erwin Panofsky, whose seminal essay, 'Gothic Architecture and Scholasticism,' was first published in 1951.[30] Initially delivered as a lecture at the Benedictine foundation of Saint Vincent's College, this text argued for the intellectual homology between the emergence of Scholastic thought in the early 13th century and the emergence of late Gothic architecture: "As the Scholastic movement, prepared by Benedictine learning [. . .] was carried on and brought to fruition by the Dominicans and Franciscans, so did the Gothic style, prepared in Benedictine monasteries [. . .] achieve its culmination in the great city churches."[31] Panofsky was not, of course, implying a direct influence of text over architecture, but rather a common state of mind that informed the architects and clergy alike, a "mental habit," similar to that ascribed by art historians to the architects, painters, and dramatists of the period they called Mannerist. And while a month after Rowe's return to Cambridge from the Dominican monastery of La Tourette, he delivered his lectures on the Gothic, in which he disavowed any literal communion between Gothic and Scholastic thought, it was certainly true that Rowe was fascinated by the parallels between a "scholastic" periodization and that of mannerism.

It is in this context that we can understand his summation of Le Corbusier's architectural method as applied to the monastery. For Rowe, the dialectic employed, as between building and site, and all the other seemingly contradictory statements in form, was "quintessentially" Dominican, "like rival protagonists of a debate who progressively contradict and clarify each other's meaning"—in sum, a "scholastic debate." Not, Rowe said, that "the architect set out deliberately to provide the plastic analog of scholastic debate." Rather, "[i]t was only that his state of mind and that of his clients were coincident in their astringent quality, and that both parties were ironically aware of their common identity and difference." The intellectual integrity of the Dominican Scholastics and that of their architect were able, as in the high Gothic moment, "to bring religious institutions and modern architecture into accord."[32]

As he wrote much later, in 1996, his stay in the convent was "an infinitely rewarding experience" and especially so because, forbidden to speak, the monks listened to long readings on "aspects of French archeology." Rowe, sensitive to the Scholastic method, was entranced to hear the voice of the reader intone references to Viollet-le-Duc and the romantic writer Prosper Mérimée, thus confirming the survival of the 19th century in the 20th, and allowing his mind to concentrate on architecture.[33]

The parallels between Panofsky's understanding of Scholastic architecture and his similar understanding of mannerist architecture as evinced in his excursus to the essay "The First Page of Giorgio Vasari's 'Libro,'" (where he explicates in an uncanny reply of Rowe's comparison of the facades of the Casa Palladio and Le Corbusier's Chaux-de-Fonds the Mannerist qualities of Domenico Becafumi's project for remodeling Casa dei Borghesi, Siena) were thus evident to Rowe, and in the essay on La Tourette, the two were finally brought together with a rhetorical confidence that would never again be repeated, at least in the exhaustive (and, in Rowe's terms, exhausting) extended excursus on a single building.

★★★

Perhaps it is impossible today to recapture a moment when history, theory, and criticism can be so integrally captured by an architectural sensibility. After the *longue durée* of analytical approaches drawn from outside the discipline, and the resulting backlash in what has been termed "post-critical" thought, Rowe's tendentiousness, his *retardataire* social posture, seems, if nothing else, dated. Yet his conviction that a building is so much more than its physical objecthood, that this very status as object might be unpacked through the detective faculty of vision, in order to reveal a complex and often dialectical argument that it at once constitutes and is constituted by, and that it is the role of criticism to unravel this argument—this might still, one hopes, hold its value in a world too quickly divided between the "authority" of facts and the vagaries of opinion.

Notes

1 I have been asked by the editor of this collection to make clear in what ways my own approaches to history, theory, and criticism take issue with those of Rowe. I have preferred to allow Rowe his own place in the field and perhaps to reclaim for him what successive developments in historiography and theory might have obscured—his potential, that is,

for the contemporary critical analysis of architecture. The following essay is a revised and much expanded version of my "Up Against the Wall: Colin Rowe at La Tourette," *Log* 24 (Winter–Spring 2012): 7–17. For a study of the origins and development of Rowe's thought and its influence on the architecture of James Stirling, see my *Histories of the Immediate Present: Inventing Architectural Modernism* (Cambridge, MA: MIT Press, 2008), chap. 2, "Mannerist Modernism," 61–106.

2 Architectural criticism, as distinct from history and theory, has always been somewhat of a hybrid, caught, as Erwin Panofsky noted, between the narrative description of the object in context and the value judgments associated with a building's status as an aesthetic object. Vasari mixed biographical anecdote with sharp critical observations to produce a ranked list of Renaissance architects that set the roster for several centuries. Johann Winckelmann tried joining a historical-style schema of development in three stages—birth, maturity, and decay—to an absolutist belief in the virtues of the "high" Greek period that condemned everything after Pericles to a slow decline. John Ruskin was so devoted to the idea of the "Gothic" (whether "Byzantine," "Romanesque," or the three periods of his "Gothic") that the Renaissance was no more than an unhappy end to art. Wölfflin's "Renaissance" was contrasted with a "Baroque" that led to the evisceration of the humanist body; Geoffrey Scott's "Renaissance" outshone all previous eras in his "Humanism." Freighted with the style wars of the 19th century, modernist architectural criticism attempted to remove itself from aesthetic opinion through the lenses of abstraction—the formal method of Wölfflin without its pathology of decadence—and scientific observation—the psychology of perception and experience. Postwar Britain inherited all of these modes, some embedded in the connoisseurial tradition inherited from the 18th century and still active in the articles of *Country Life*, and, in a more scholarly vein, in the Courtauld Institute with Anthony Blunt, some derived from the formal painterly criticism of Roger Fry and the psychological interpretation of Adrian Stokes and some animated by the Marxist readings of Francis Klingender and Herbert Read. This landscape was, however, quickly transformed by the arrival of the German scholars in exile—notably Rudolf Wittkower and Nikolaus Pevsner. Wittkower's influence was exercised through the equally recent transplant of the Warburg Institute from 1934 to 1956 before his departure for Columbia University; Pevsner's was long-lasting, first in his editorship of the *Architectural Review* and then in the apparently inexhaustible series of the *Buildings of England*, as he opportunistically translated his earlier Germanophilia into Anglophilia.

3 Colin Rowe, "Thanks to the RIBA," *The Journal of Architecture* 1 (Spring 1996): 8.

4 Ibid.

5 Reyner Banham, *New Society*, March 17, 1966, reviewing Douglas Stephen, Kenneth Frampton, and Michael Carpetian, *British Buildings, 1960–1964* (London: A. and C. Black, 1965), cited by Alexander Caragonne, "Editor's Note" to Caragonne, ed. Colin Rowe, *As I Was Saying: Recollections and Miscellaneous Essays*, vol. 1 (Cambridge, MA: MIT Press, 1996), ix. As Caragonne points out, Banham's outburst against Rowe as occasioned not by the book in question but by its dedication to Rowe—a preemptive attack against Rowe's potential candidacy for director of the Architectural Association.

6 Colin Rowe, "James Stirling: A Highly Personal and Very Disjointed Memoir," in *James Stirling: Buildings and Projects*, ed. Peter Arnell and Ted Bickford (New York: Rizzoli, 1984), 10.

7 Ibid., 11. For a comprehensive and incisive summary of the politics of Rowe's positions toward modernist utopianism and his "formalism" as compared to that of Clement Greenberg, see Joan Ockman, "Form without Utopia: Contextualizing Colin Rowe," *Journal of the Society of Architectural Historians* 57, no. 4 (December 1998): 448–56.

8 For a comprehensive analysis of this circle, and an in-depth study of Scott, see Mark Campbell, "A Beautiful Leisure" (PhD diss., Princeton University, 2013).

9 Rowe, *As I Was Saying*, vol. 1, 10.

10 Rowe, "Thanks to the RIBA," 8.

11 Rowe, "Addendum 1973," in *The Mathematics of the Ideal Villa and Other Essays* (Cambridge, MA: MIT Press, 1976), 16.

12 Ibid.

13 Rowe was never a great lover of footnotes. Apart from a couple of references to Frances Yates in his MA thesis for London University, all of the rest refer to historical treatises. More importantly, there were no acknowledgments of his advisor, Rudolf Wittkower (whose two articles on Palladio in the *Journal of the Warburg and Coutauld Institutes* are listed in the bibliography of the thesis) in the subsequent articles, "The Mathematics of the Ideal Villa" and "Mannerism and Modern Architecture," both of which were deeply dependent on his teacher's published works. Indeed, the only two references given in the latter piece were to Nikolaus Pevsner and Anthony Blunt, ignoring Wittkower's groundbreaking articles on Michelangelo's Laurentian Library and Carlo Rainaldi, written in the 1930s but the substance of which must have been communicated to his English students. Despite this, Wittkower himself, in writing his 1953 essay "Inigo Jones, Architect and Man of Letters," largely based on Rowe's research, was generous enough to note, "A pupil of mine, Colin Rowe, has substantiated [the assumption that Jones was preparing an architectural treatise] in a brilliant but not yet published thesis." Rowe did add a footnote to the republication of "The Mathematics of the Ideal Villa," in 1976, although referring to Wittkower's *Architectural Principles in the Age of Humanism*, which had been published two years after the first appearance of Rowe's essay. Nor was Rowe especially interested in explaining his approaches to history and criticism. There are precious few references to previous historians or to their methods in his writings: only Henry Russell Hitchcock gains a full essay, more conversational than methodological, but giving him credit for changing his mind about Frank Lloyd Wright.

14 Heinrich Wölfflin, *Principles of Art History: The Problem of the Development of Style in Later Art*, trans. M.D. Hottinger (New York: Dover Editions, 1950).

15 Ibid., 73.

16 For a developed treatment of Winckelmann's descriptive art and its influence on art history, see my *The Writing of the Walls: Architectural Theory in the Late Enlightenment*, chap. 8, "The Aesthetics of History: Winckelmann and the Greek Ideal" (Princeton, NJ: Princeton Architectural Press, 1987), 125–137, and 216n8.

17 Ibid., 128. A century later Karl Justi was to revive this description of description as an essential element in the writing of art history: Winckelmann's "descriptions are not objective in those in the natural sciences, where the author uses exhaustive terminology in an effort to be adequate to his subject-matter" but rather "a conversion of an impression received by the mind in a moment of sacred contemplation, into a series of images and concepts, just as the artist gradually converts his creative intuition into plastic reality." Karl Justi, *Winckelmann und seine Zeitgenossen* (1972), vol. 1, 45f., quoted in Max Dessoir, *Aesthetics and Theory of Art* (1906; Detroit, MI: Wayne State University Press, 1970), 407.

18 See Stephen Kite, "Architecture as Virtù: Adrian Stokes, Ezra Pound and the Ethics of 'Patterned Energy,'" *The Journal of Architecture* 6 (Spring 2001): 81–95.

19 Colin Rowe, "Dominican Monastery of La Tourette, Eveux-sur-Arbresie, Lyons," *Architectural Review* (June 1961): 400–10.

20 José Ortega y Gasset, *Meditations on Don Quixote* [1914], trans. Evelyn Rugg and Diego Martin (New York: W.W. Norton, 1961), 68–69. This book, published in translation in 1961, was perhaps the inspiration if not the confirmation of Rowe's thesis.

21 Rowe, "Dominican Monastery," 401.

22 The phrase, "The elements of the site rise up like walls panoplied in the power of their cubic coefficient, stratification, material, etc., like the walls of the room," was omitted from the Corbusier quotation in the original essay but inserted when it was republished in 1976. *Mathematics and Other Essays*, 186.

23 Rowe, "Dominican Monastery," 401.

24 Ibid., 401.

25 Ibid., 402.

26 Ibid.

27 Colin Rowe, "Mannerism and Modern Architecture," *Architectural Review* (May 1950): 292.

28 Rowe, "Dominican Monastery," 407.

29 Rowe, "La Tourette," in *The Mathematics of the Ideal Villa and Other Essays*, 196–200. Rowe inserted three pages on the subject of "Le Corbusier's passion for walls," in this republication of his "Dominican Monastery" article.

30 Erwin Panofsky, *Gothic Architecture and Scholasticism: An Inquiry into the Analogy of the Arts, Philosophy, and Religion in the Middle Ages* (New York: Meridian Books, 1957).

31 Panofsky, *Gothic Architecture*, 22.

32 Rowe, "Dominican Monastery," 408–09.

33 As Rowe wrote in 1996 in the prologue to the republication of his extended essay on "The Provocative Façade" (1987), "My three days at La Tourette were spent in thinking about its relations to Maison Domino, Maison Citrohan, to Garches and to Poissy; and the side wall of Maison Citrohan, promoted to prominence, has obsessed me ever since." Rowe, *As I Was Saying*, vol. 2, ed. Alexander Caragonne (Cambridge, MA: MIT Press, 1996), 172.

"[Rowe's own personal prejudices] would increasingly color his vision in the years to come. These were anti-zeitgeist, anti-historicism, anti-scientism, anti-utopian, anti-ideal, and many others. As these became more strident after 1975, when *Collage City* and figure/ground reversals became tied to Rome (witness Roma Interrotta of 1978) and his more classical precedents, Rowe's work became almost indistinguishable from the historicist nostalgia that only several years earlier he was critiquing ..."

BIFURCATING ROWE[1]

Peter Eisenman

One of the indelible memories of my travels with Colin Rowe in the summer of 1961 was in front of the first Palladian villa I saw, the villa Montagnana. It was hot, dusty, and humid all at the same time. Rowe sat drinking a San Pellegrino Aranciata (much better than Fanta, although at the time, Recoaro was another favored brand) as I stood in the sun in 35-degree-plus heat. Rowe implored, "Tell me something about what you are looking at that you cannot see!" In other words, not the material rustication, not the three stories, and not the front portico symmetry. I was initially totally confused, because architecture for me had always been about what was seen; its presence in real built material. Although there were drawings and models of the Palladian villas, Colin and I spent an entire three months looking at what existed!

While today the idea of the "presence of the unseen" remains a central tenet of my own work, it can be said to be one of the two major problematics in understanding Rowe's thought—both then and now. In order to contextualize what is to follow, it must first be said that Rowe and Manfredo Tafuri, for different reasons, remain the two major critical voices of the last half of the twentieth century; if one must include Reyner Banham, then Rowe would be one of three. And second, the two issues I discuss here—the notions of close reading and the synthetic project—can be said to still relate to the premises of architectural thought today.

A close reading is what animated Rowe's two early essays, "The Mathematics of the Ideal Villa" and "Mannerism and Modern Architecture"; one can say that what close reading is to writing, the "presence of an absence" is to architecture—including a Palladian villa. This concerned Rowe's ability to collapse two disparate ideas in time, space, and style and to produce in a text, as if by magic, what had previously been unseen in the analysis of an architectural work—in his case, mostly Le Corbusier and Palladio. Rowe imagined how a building could be construed when seen in new and different contexts; in other words, he liked to imagine the unseen: his process of formal analysis implied knowing something that was not simply visible. And this meant that things and their history were never what they seemed to be—so-called facts—but rather possible subjects of invention, as well as questions of value. For example, I am reminded of Rowe's repeated insistence on the capriciousness of history. If the Genoese, he used to say, had sold Corsica to Great Britain instead of the French in 1764, Napoleon Bonaparte, who was born in 1769, would never have been able to attend the Royal Military Academy at Sandhurst in England, because the English had class restrictions for entry. Instead, little Napoleon was able to enter the Ecole Militaire in Paris because no such class restrictions existed in France; and the rest, as Rowe would say, is history.

In his early essays, he practiced a form of close reading which might still be useful today for its inventive nature; indeed, the methods of close reading typical of the formal analyses known from the theory of the 1970s and 1980s seem to have lost their capacity to come to terms with the reading requirements of today's digital culture in architecture. In fact, many people would argue that close reading in the era of the digital 2.0 has become altogether quaint. For example, one can ask what kind of close reading is possible when a single algorithm can generate 50,000 variables? How one chooses in such a context has little to do with close reading. Or what to make of decision making by crowd sourcing?

Clearly, close reading is an individual activity, but to understand why and how Rowe's project may seem to be an anachronism today, it is necessary to go back to another equally important early essay of his, "Character and Composition," which was written in the late 1950s but could not find a publisher until the second issue of *Oppositions* in the early 1970s. While the essay involved a shift in Rowe's manner of close reading, it also revealed an aspect of Rowe's project that may have been previously overlooked.

First, one must consider Rowe's definition of the term *composition*, which today has fostered many deviations, and many of which have little resonance with Rowe's definition. This would include both diagrammatic analysis and textual analysis. For example, a diagram is a template for the production of something that does not pre-exist its notation; perhaps, it captures the unseen, whereas composition is the process that takes an a priori idea about form and brings it to some condition of realization.

Second, the diagram can be conceived as the *parti* of a building, but in many quarters the diagram is pure program—much like the bubble diagrams of the Bauhaus, which is all content and no form.

In Rowe's essay, composition is construed as a planimetric idea, whereas the notion of character relates to the vertical plane or facade. The essence of his belief in what one can call the "Albertian synthetic project" is the possible union of these two, whereby the qualities of the picturesque become an effect that is essentially compositional. While Rowe's analysis of this phenomenon in his essay is limited to a narrative of nineteenth-century English houses, it is not this quality alone which distinguishes its theoretical biases from the two earlier texts. Rather, it is two other examples which open up a much deeper problematic in Rowe's oeuvre, and that would permanently move Rowe's work away from the ahistorical character of his earlier close readings. These two would be the introduction to the second edition of his *Five Architects* book as well as his project for the "Roma Interrotta" exhibition of 1978. In each of these contexts, Rowe exhibits hostility to modernism; modernism became, for him, the mixing of a scientism in the form of the zeitgeist with history understood as historicism—a quality that was problematic in his reading of Karl Popper's *The Poverty of Historicism.*

Rowe has stated on many occasions that modern architecture could never be a synthetic project because its *morale* and its *physique* (his terms for ideology and form, respectively) were not to be equated. This was the critique that he used in his introduction to *Five Architects* in 1975. Clearly, without a morale, the physique promoted by the Five Architects was forms of a latent zeitgeist.

The Roma Interrotta project of 1978 then was a different sort of speculation, being a poignant moment in Rowe's quest for a non-modern urbanism. This quest became known as "contextualism" and provoked an entirely different idea of urban intervention largely seen through the lens of figure/ground, meaning black-and-white drawings similar to those found in the Nolli Map of Rome of 1748. These figure/ground reversals, which read like early gestalt psychology's ink blots, sparked Rowe's interest in the figured object, and it was much more inflected than simple exedra forms (which he used to call "catchers mitts"). This interest moved Rowe early on to complex urban form, in particular to mega-buildings, such as the Munich Residenz and the Hofburg Palace in Vienna. In fact, it was a mistaken belief that O. Matthias Ungers shared similar interest in urban mega-buildings that brought him to Ithaca. These found figural forms, taken "out-of-context," generated Rowe's idea

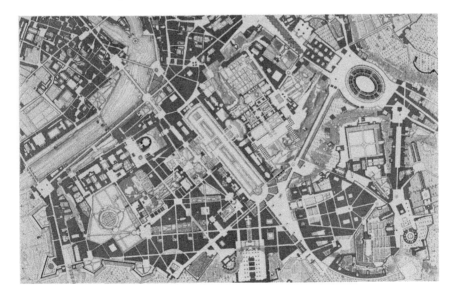

FIGURE 11 Colin Rowe, Judith Di Maio, Peter Carl, and Steven Peterson, "Roma Interrotta" contribution, Sector VIII of Nolli map of Rome from 1748 (1978)

Credit: Courtesy Steven Peterson and Barbara Littenberg

COLLAGE CITY

Colin Rowe and Fred Koetter

FIGURE 12   Cover of Colin Rowe and Fred Koetter's *Collage City* (1978)

Credit: Courtesy of MIT Press, Cambridge

of collage. A fundamental generator of Rowe's contextual strategy were (what Rowe would call) set pieces or archetypal configurations, which acquired a new definition and existence in their context.

But there is still something that cannot be explained through questioning Rowe's rational arguments and that is his personal belief system, or ideology, which is seemingly masked in his *belles-lettres* style of writing. It might well become most clear in his introduction to the *Five Architects* book of 1972 and 1975. While for the sake of propriety (he was supposedly friends with each one of the Five), writers do not, as a rule, critique the authors for whom the introduction is written. Rowe says his critique, in a thinly veiled excuse, was to cover a potential critique by others of the pure formalism exhibited by the projects in the book. But since he himself says the morale of modern architecture, its ideology, was already exhausted, the only reason for its physique (its forms) was because of their unusual staying power. He cited cubism and related aspects of early-twentieth-century painting as the only viable and sustaining reason for what was displayed in the book. But, since the Five never argued for the morale of modern architecture, no less in their own work, this must have actually been Rowe's own argument. Rowe was already on record as being against the modern because there was never any possibility, despite its claims, for a synthesis of physique and morale. So his argument as a supposed cover against any future critique by others of the Five was actually Rowe's own cover-up for all of his own personal prejudices; and those would increasingly color his vision in the years to come. These were anti-zeitgeist, anti-historicism, anti-scientism, anti-utopian, anti-ideal, and many others. As these became more strident after 1975, when *Collage City* and figure/ground reversals became tied to Rome (witness Roma Interrotta of 1978) and his more classical precedents, Rowe's work became almost indistinguishable from the historicist nostalgia that only several years earlier he was critiquing (as he did in his "Yale Mathematics Building" essay). Rowe's arguments were no longer about seeing the unseen but rather the reality of a now-prized set of formal manipulations that suited his ultimately Tory tastes.

As the historical time of mannerism was an attempt to redirect the satisfied energy of the successes of the early sixteenth century, so too are the formal experimentations today an outgrowth of the successes of modernism often requiring a different form of close reading. Would Rowe have been able to adjust to the present digital explosions or would his hostility to what he would believe as an overdetermined response to today keep him well apart? The question that must be asked is, as today's discourse is unfolding, which Rowe would survive: the close reading of the unseen or the conservative leanings of his own temperaments? Or maybe the bifurcation is between the individual Rowe and his avatar Rowe-bots. Future histories will be left to judge.

Note

1   This title comes from one of my favorite "Rowe-isms." When traveling in my Volkswagen Bug in the summers of 1961–1962, Rowe would always say "at the next bifurcation," when "the next fork" would have done equally well.

Opposing Zeitgeist

"[Rowe] did not understand the *Zeitgeist* he talked so much about and preferred to retire to his 'Monticello' in Ithaca. . . . I left Berlin in 1968 to take the position [as chairman at Cornell] with the surprising effect that Colin, who I thought was my friend and with whom I shared so many views in architecture, turned completely against me—calling me a Marxist and undermining my position wherever he could."

HE WHO DID NOT UNDERSTAND THE ZEITGEIST

O. Mathias Ungers

I do not remember any more when I met Colin Rowe for the first time: it was either 1964 or 1965. But I remember very well that it was in Berlin. I had just started to teach at the Technical University in Berlin. I worked with the students on the problem of morphology in architecture. The morphological transformation of forms and elements was one of the main concerns of our studies. It was a field in architecture based on studies of Durand and on Wittkower's writings on Palladianism. We published the result of our work in a self-published magazine called *Publications on Architecture (Veröffentlichungen zur Architektur)*.

Anybody who knows Colin can imagine that based on his own interest and background, he was most interested in these studies—especially in the question of transformation. Our work was very closely related to his own urban studies of transformation, which he applied to various cities in the United States. I do not remember why he came to Berlin and who invited him, but he knew about our work and seemed to be very impressed by it. We had a very harmonic and inspiring time in Berlin. Particularly the work of two students, Rainer Jagals and Eckardt Reisinger, impressed him very much, and he was eager to take copies of their work back to Cornell with him. He also made known our publication on architecture—for which there was not much interest in Berlin because of the hegemony of the Scharoun group, but at Cornell he had prepared the intellectual ground for it.

The meeting in Berlin led to my invitation as a visiting critic to Cornell. I arrived in Ithaca for the first time in 1966, and offered a four-week course in design, working on similar problems as with the students in Berlin. The work had to do with basic questions of form, mutation, and an elementary language of architecture independent of time and location. It had to do with the autonomy of architecture—of architecture as a function of nothing else than the logic of form and space. In other words, it was the philosophy of rationalism, that is, the idea that the "ratio" of

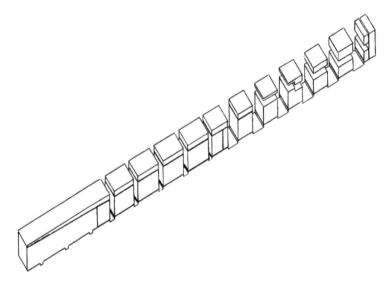

FIGURE 13   Rainer Jagals, Hommage à O.M.U. (1967)

Credit: Courtesy Galerie Strecker, Rainer Jagals, exhibit catalogue, Dezember 1967–Februar 1968, Berlin

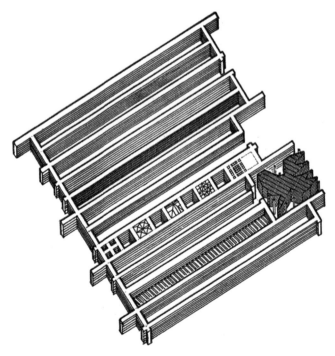

FIGURE 14   Rainer Jagals, Untitled, 30 × 19 cm (1967)

Credit: Courtesy Galerie Strecker, Rainer Jagals, exhibit catalogue, Dezember 1967–Februar 1968, Berlin

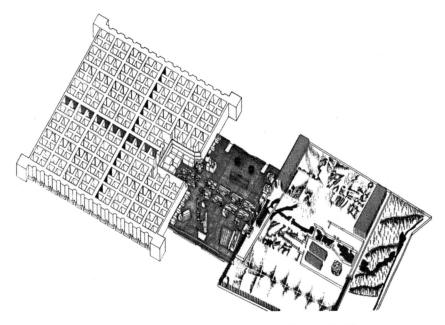

FIGURE 15 Rainer Jagals, Necropolis, isometric, 90.5 × 138 cm (1967)

Credit: Courtesy Galerie Strecker, Rainer Jagals, exhibit catalogue, Dezember 1967–Februar 1968, Berlin

architecture is architecture itself. My course was well accepted, not least because of Colin. For that reason the work in Cornell was quite an intellectual pleasure for me, although I never felt entirely comfortable—coming from the metropolitan environment of Berlin, which was full of tensions, to the country-squire environment of upstate New York.

After my first excursion to a place I had never heard of before, I met Colin a second time in Berlin. Architectural theory had completely disappeared in the minds of students and teachers in Germany due to the exodus of most of the influential people to America in the 1930s. Motivated by the great German tradition in architectural theory at the end of the 19th and beginning of the 20th century, I intended to renew this tradition, and decided to organize an international congress on architectural theory in Berlin. I wanted to revive the theoretical line of men such as Sörgel, Lipps, Semper, Wölfflin, Sitte, Hildebrand, Schmarsow, Riese, Worringer, Simmel, Frey, Behne, and others. The congress took place in December of 1967 with the title "Theory in Architecture: An International Congress in Berlin." Most of the leading theoreticians at that time participated in the congress—including Reyner Banham, Lucius Burckhardt, Kenneth Frampton, Sigfried Giedion, Julius Posener, Eduard Sekler, and Adolf Max Vogt. Colin was also among the speakers. His speech was entitled "The Crisis in the Cultural Cabinet"—one of Colin's typical and provocative titles and a critical consideration of Banham. He spoke, as usual, in a very

FIGURE 16 *Spiegel* Cover 24/1967, "The Revolting Students of Berlin"
Credit: SPIEGEL 24/1967

sophisticated way about the question of technology versus *Zeitgeist*, which was at the same time very inspiring and far over the heads of the German students.

The congress was a disaster. This was in 1967—the beginning of the students' revolution, which reached its peak in 1968. The students' interest was entirely political;

they were not interested at all in a theoretical architectural discourse. Colin had no sympathy for the students' political activities and was pretty much disgusted by their—as he thought—rather stupid reaction. Giedion (poor man) was booed at because nobody wanted to listen to his explanation of his three basic spatial concepts and a presentation of his latest book. The auditorium was filled with at least 2,000 protesting students, whose interest was not in any way in theoretical, historical, or conceptual architectural problems. They were politically motivated and wanted to change society as a whole. The congress ended after two days with a massive student protest; they unrolled a banner with the slogan "Every building is beautiful. Stop building." Instead of listening to the masters, they stormed the final panel, yelling, screaming, and chasing the speakers out of the auditorium. This was the end of all discourse on architecture in Germany and the beginning of the Ho Chi Minh demonstrations in Berlin.

Colin and all the others were speechless. They could not believe the violence they had been exposed to. He left Berlin, and I think the shock was so profound that he, as much as I know, never wanted to come back. He did not understand the *Zeitgeist* he talked so much about and preferred to retire to his "Monticello" in Ithaca; he returned to his books and his humanist lifestyle as a "country squire" with friendly students at his feet who listened in peace and harmony. He was disgusted by the vicious and aggressive political world outside. He was a completely apolitical man who did not want to be confronted with the mob on the street.

What happened thereafter? Cornell was looking for a new chairman. I think it was Colin who was quite instrumental in bringing me to Cornell as chairman. I left Berlin in 1968 to take the position with the surprising effect that Colin, who I thought was my friend and with whom I shared so many views in architecture, turned completely against me—calling me a Marxist and undermining my position wherever he could. In other words, he turned into an enemy—not so much personally, though I was very disappointed to experience the change in his character, but intellectually. I found Colin's influence on students quite dangerous because it was overpowering. He did not allow students to develop their own minds but successfully and sometimes even cynically indoctrinated them.

As head of the department and as more or less a product of Humboldt's idea of an encyclopedic and humanistic view on education, I felt obliged to let every student find their own way instead of becoming a product of somebody else's dogmatic view. As a teacher, Colin did not make the students free in their own mind, but he monopolized them with his dogmatic views on architecture and urban design, where he believed himself to be an exclusive expert. He never acted alone but was always surrounded by admiring fellows who acted like him, spoke like him, and were lost when he was not around. He saw himself more as a messiah, surrounded by his pupils, than as a teacher who could learn from the students' curiosity and questions—as, for example, Louis Kahn did.

Not least because of Colin, the Cornell experience ended for me in great disillusionment. I had difficulties to bear the monastic narrowness in upstate New York,

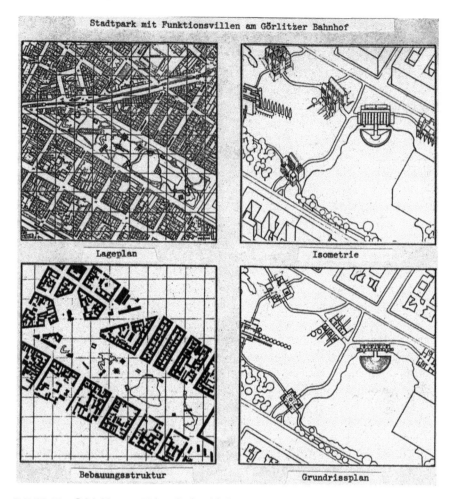

Stadtpark mit Funktionsvillen am Görlitzer Bahnhof

Lageplan

Isometrie

Bebauungsstruktur

Grundrissplan

FIGURE 17 O.M. Ungers, Urban Park with Representation Villas near Görlitz Train Station (1977)

Credit: With the permission of Ungers Archiv für Architekturwissenschaften UAA, Cologne

From: O.M. Ungers. *The City in the City—Berlin: A Green Archipelago* (1977)

which he had created and where he played the role of the abbot. I left Ithaca in 1980 after having taught a studio in architectural design parallel to Colin's urban design studio; mine were attended by people such as Rem Koolhaas and Hans Kollhoff. I went back to the world of building and never returned.

Despite all the controversy that developed in our relationship, I think Colin not only continued the 19th-century tradition of the great thinkers in the field of theory in architecture with his writings and his academic work. His position as a highly intellectual and most sophisticated theoretician is beyond any doubts. His influence on thinking in architecture in the second half of the 20th century was enormously important in the United States and begins slowly to draw awareness and interest in Europe.

In my life as an architect, Colin played a major role, and I would not like to have missed the various meetings, encounters, as well as the sustained discussions on architecture with him. He was an ideal counterpart for my own thinking in architecture.

"[Rowe's and Adorno's] aesthetic of fragments did not engender the new 'new world' they so ardently pursued. And yet, Colin would not be satisfied with the Cornell studio projects, nor would Adorno find fulfillment in a purely serial musical world. And that is due to the fact that literary criticism can be no more literature than architectural criticism can be architecture. It may bring down walls, but it will not build the new house or the new city, let alone a new country or continent."

UNRESOLVED ENCOUNTERS WITH COLIN ROWE

Léon Krier

Not long before his disappearance, Colin Rowe sat through a lecture of mine, alone, hieratic, in a wheelchair, on the upper gangway of the amphitheater, silent, silhouetted against the darkened hall by a low security light. Later in a restaurant, for some mysterious reason, we were unable to get the old conversation going. His blue eyes filled with suppressed questions and unutterable angst. It was a melancholy occasion, and I had a long, unfinished letter to him waiting on my desk when I heard of his death.

After several months of digging my brain for what possibly I could write on or around Colin Rowe I am left with a feeling of regret and frustration, similar to what I sensed on the many occasions I had tried, vainly, to talk to him "seriously," for example, on subjects that imperatively needed to be addressed and that even my best friends and colleagues preferred to ignore. At the time I was desperate to find somebody of caliber, and Rowe was a choice candidate. According to James Stirling, we were meant to get along. And yet the house never caught fire short of inflammable material, I suppose. Rowe invariably defeated attempts at rapprochement with so many diversions, monologizing on subjects or royalty of remote places and times in which I had no interest. Also he regularly enjoyed ranting against "Rationalismus" and "Marxismus"—doctrines he had convinced himself had irredeemably corrupted me; it was a pointless worry. I had felt no lasting temptation in either direction. Rowe's lecture at the Bartlett had cured me of the last traces of utopian leanings.

Giving me more credit than I actually deserved with the "Tendenza" and the Italian Left, Colin had put me in an ideological corner and would not let me out. Nor did he seem to have the slightest interest in hearing my story *de viva voce*. I was never interested in the Moscow-oriented power politics of Rossi or Tafuri, or in Gregotti's cloned monsters, or in Soviet or capitalist-type mass industrialization of building elements. I always abhorred card-carrying group disciplines of any kind, and I was not a dotty groupie of Stirling, Ungers, or anyone else. The "Rational Architecture" exhibition and symposium I had organized in London and Barcelona in 1975 was specifically intended as a corrective to the "*Architettura Razionale*" exhibition in Milan; the notion "rational" architecture was too good to be wasted on Rossi's exhibition, which I felt had little to offer in defining a new direction. Rossi's Triennale was nothing but a mixed bag of architectural pin-ups without any common reason (or rhyme). Instead, I invited architects not because of their personal "*griffe*," or signature, but because within their often disparate work, I identified elements which responded to the typological and morphological order of the European city; there was no doubt in my mind that the European city was being sacrificed to the agenda

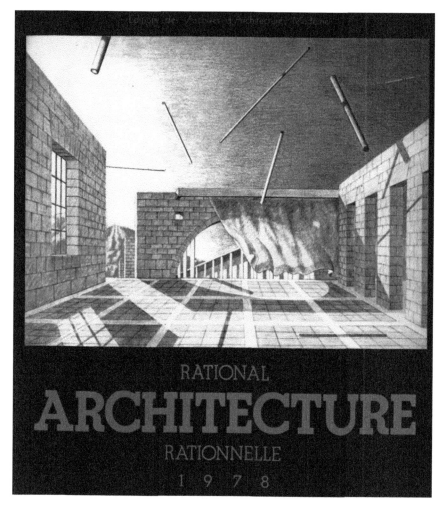

FIGURE 18 Cover page of *Rational Architecture: The Reconstruction of the European City* (1978)

Credit: Courtesy of Archives d'Architecture Moderne, asbl, Brussels

of the *Charter Of Athens*. In that context, the projects I had pulled together could be seen as the undeclared avant-garde for the reconstruction of the European city. O. Mathias Ungers was scandalized that I had not exhibited the many projects he had submitted and that I regarded as soul-killing slums for the masses. Instead I had copied out of magazines three outstanding earlier projects he had by then condemned as *démodé*—"*überholt*," as he said.

Colin feared that I was propelled by millenarist utopianism, whereas my main motivation was simply to understand, retrieve, and give a contemporary legitimacy to the extraordinary traditional architectural and urban environment I had grown up in. I had by that time traveled, studied, and experienced enough comparable material to surmise the categorical superiority of traditional architecture over modernist theories and developments. I had produced for the *AAM Magazine* in Brussels a series of articles, titled "Private Virtue and Public Vice," in which I documented the fact that famous avant-gardists around the world lived, worked, retired, and vacationed in traditional architectural and urban environs while propagating modernist utopias for the common man. One of Colin's staple subjects of conversation was to rhapsodize about the best place to retire. This would invariably be an old property in the Tuscan hills backing onto some old *casale*.

It was somewhat ironic that I had admired in Ungers those very same projects, which made Colin appoint him to Cornell. But then, we were both equally appalled by Ungers's post-1966 pedagogy and work. In his first years of teaching at the Technical University of Berlin, Ungers had surrounded himself with a small group of intelligent and very talented assistants—including Ulrich Flemming, Jürgen Sawade, Volker Sayn, Johann-Friedrich Geist, Michael Wegener, Franz Oswald, and the unequaled Wolf Meyer-Christian. During three happy years they formed a loose squadron, and each one of these individuals produced stellar work. However, when Ungers settled at Cornell, that collective genius had not traveled with him. It had evaporated, never to recover; the magic was gone. And Colin's pruning experiment not only failed but also poisoned the Cornell tree and the rich harvest he had rightfully expected.

I did not know Rowe as a man of debate or dialogue, nor would he be lectured to. He never directly reacted to an argument, but would invariably divert into other—often trivial—subjects "ta ta ta . . . but Leon, Leon, Leon, Leon—he would say, you forget that the Countess of Y. was hopelessly infatuated with Prince Consort and *Wagnerschule*," and on and on. I also tried to introduce Colin to P.L. Cervellati's sophisticated conservation policy for the historical center of Bologna, but he would just wave "ta ta ta . . ." and switch off.

When Ungers invited me to teach at Cornell, Stirling warned me before I left London that this would seal the end of my relationship with Colin. However, I hadn't even set down my luggage at the Heller House when I found Colin's card inviting Massimo Scolari and me to dinner that same evening. He was going to pick us up in his Beetle. Already in the car, he launched a diatribe against Ungers as if I were to fatally fall prey to Mathias's irresistible propositions. In fact, Ungers pressed me every single day to work with him on his very uninspired Cologne Museum

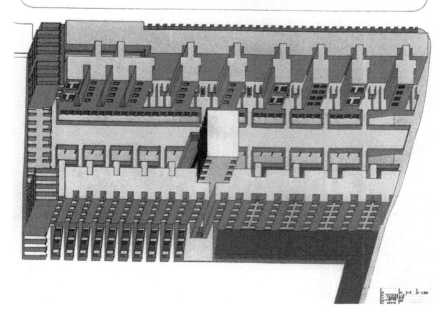

FIGURE 19 O.M. Ungers, Köln-Zollstock Grünzug-Süd (1962–64)

Credit: Courtesy of Ungers Archiv für Architekturwissenschaften UAA, Cologne

competition. I would, I joked, only if he went back to what he had been doing ten years before. "That's long finished, *vorbei, erledigt . . .*" He kept hammering. "What I am doing now is *so viel besser, weiiiiit überlegen* [so much better, very superior], *mein lieber Leon.* The only one I fear now is Stirling," he added. He clearly had a sense that Stirling and he formed the lonesome peak of the profession.

The trenches at Cornell were dug in deep on both sides by the time I got there in September 1975. Notwithstanding Colin's and Jim's warnings, I was interested in talking with Ungers about his projects of 1960–67, from Grünzug-Süd to Tiergarten Museum, to find out why he departed from this line of thinking and designing and maybe to get him back on course. Absurdly, Ungers had abandoned the very ideas that had brought him to Cornell, and the isolation between the opposing camps became total. Doors were shut, and I did not come across any of the famous Cornell Studio work. In fact, I had no idea that such work ever existed. Colin didn't mention it, nor was I invited to attend studios or juries. Koolhaas had by then left Ithaca and the Institute for Architecture and Urban Studies (IAUS). I knew his work because we met privately in London through Elia Zenghelis—the cofounder and mentor of OMA. I found Madelon Vriesendorp's illustrations delightful, but Rem's ideas on New York City bizarre at best.

When looking at my sketches for Derby, Stirling once remarked, "This is the kind of thing Colin is doing in Cornell," but it went no further than that. Stirling kept inviting me to dinner with Colin, with Alan Colquhoun and Ken Frampton, among

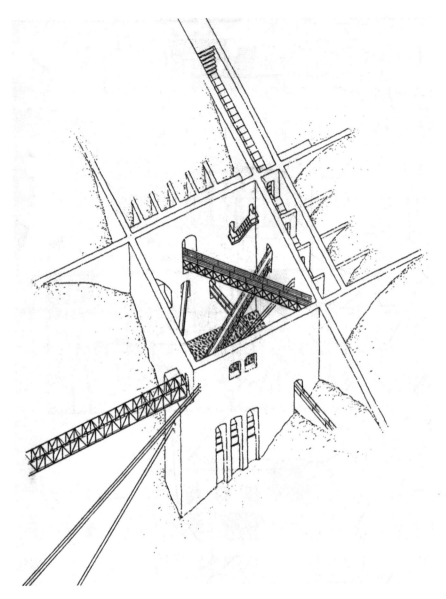

FIGURE 20   Léon Krier, *Difficult Access to O.M.U.* (1975)

Credit: © Léon Krier

others, but these were cult evenings rather than debating sessions. The issue of classicism was not seriously addressed except when talking about furniture—particularly Thomas Hope. David Watkin's monograph was an inspiration to all, and it was the only book Stirling ever lent me to read.[1] Colin had entrusted me as keeper of an extraordinary neoclassical chaise. I very shyly tried out some classical details for

Derby and Siemens, but Stirling would not warm to them. My monumental steps and arcade were replaced in the very last moment by the signature patent glazing curtain wall. By then I was thoroughly disillusioned with modernism and the unspeakably crude urban theories associated with it. I took a deep plunge without knowing too well what I was doing when I worked on my Echternach project. Stirling commented that he "wouldn't dare go that far." He would rather cling to industrial aesthetics, which to me remained poorly argued and poorly worked out. Particularly with the projects for St. Andrews, Runcorn, and the Cambridge History Library, we all knew in the office about the impending fiasco; that it all was industrial looks with little technological substance. It became evident in the later projects for Stuttgart and Düsseldorf that my minimalist neoclassical doodles triggered something in Stirling after I had left the office. These sketches were known and exhibited in the narrow circle of the Institute for Architecture and Urban Studies and in Princeton in 1975 as the "LK coloring book" and were published by *Controspazio, Architectural Design, Architecture d'Aujourd'hui, Casabella,* and *Lotus* from 1972 onward.

When in 1977 Anthony Vidler invited me to Princeton to stand in for his sabbatical, Michael Graves, who had by then an interest in neoclassical architecture close to my own, insisted that he and I teach together. "Rather stay friends" was my reply, knowing that the Princeton School of Architecture was a "Michael Graves school," in which everyone—both his friends and his enemies—lingered two years behind his own stylistic evolution. Even though by the fall of 1977 Michael was doing neoclassical experiments, they were not released for general imitation yet. Preceding that, Graves and Eisenman had taken Rowe and Slutzky's "Transparency: Part II" to the poetical extremes; by my arrival, they were still the official Princeton Architecture School maniera.

I proposed a studio on the urbanism of Le Corbusier's Mundaneum project in Geneva, but Michael didn't warm to it. I intended to develop with the students an urban architecture that would go beyond the "Five Points of Architecture" and establish a Corbusian grammar, which would distinguish between the monumental and the domestic and the classical and the vernacular. In fact, I had hoped at some point that Colin would address these critical differences, but he never did. The task still lies ahead. Failing that, I gave the students a program for locating the new Institut Français d'Architecture on the tip of the Ile St Louis in Paris. The program was drafted with Maurice Culot, who was the inaugural director of an institution just founded by President Giscard D'Estaing. Colin and I discussed turning this into an international competition but excluding French architects who, we agreed, at that moment in time were the worst in the world.

When my students wouldn't comply with the stylistic prerequisite of the Graves school, tensions became unbearable. From then on, we ran separate studios. I still wish we had "rather stayed friends." Our common jury was a disaster. Michael just was not prepared to tolerate or even discuss student work that did not comply with the established Graves line. On the following day, a snowstorm in the Appalachians stopped me in mid-journey from attending Colin's jury at Cornell. I have never been invited back to Princeton or Ithaca since.

Ungers, Rowe, and Graves had each established their own academic spheres of influence, and except for common juries, there was no serious debate or exchange. However, Rowe was the uncontested guide and guru. The lack of a coherent theory in such an intelligent and talented milieu was, in my opinion, his doing—whether intentional or not. This absence of a consistent theory left the terrain open for post-modernist Kitsch of the soft- or hard-core kind.

Neither Cornell, nor Princeton or Yale had created a platform for a debate that stepped outside the tenets of modernist urbanism and architecture. Paradoxically only Peter Eisenman's IAUS in New York, its *Oppositions* journal and the Architectural Association in London had championed eclectic doctrinaire positions. Yet few of the protagonists were aware of the fragility and uniqueness of these platforms.

With François Mitterrand elected French president, the modernist revival took center stage in European architectural debates; at that point neither the ideas of "rational architecture" nor those transmitted by Prince Charles could seriously affect what I can only describe as an ideological tsunami, which swept education and cultural politics on local and international levels. No one in the circle of critical-theoretical academia, including Rowe, had seen it coming. Under the deanship of Jaquelin Robertson, the School of Architecture in Charlottesville became briefly the place of resistance around 1980. Colin maintained a remarkable influence there, as well as in the various universities and summer schools where he taught after his retirement. Many of his students and assistants were encouraged by him to take the step which eventually led to New Urbanism and to the traditional and classical courses in Miami under Duany and Plater-Zyberk, at Portland under Lucien Steil, at Notre Dame under Thomas Gordon Smith, at Syracuse under Jean Francois Gabriel, at College Park under Steve Hurtt, and eventually at Yale under Robert A.M. Stern.

I was neither a pupil nor a peer of Colin's, and even though our relationship was always cordial, we were not friends. I made a last attempt in 1984 to collaborate with him on a common project, when Dan Cruickshank invited me to work on a proposal for redeveloping the South-Bank Arts complex to be published as a cover story in Deyan Sujic's *Blueprint*. This proposal was meant to give short shrift to Cedric Price's Commissioned Report for saving the blighted area by merely installing a mile length of (Central Park–type) public benches. Colin had put out feelers to come back to England after retiring from Cornell. I thought this was a splendid occasion to catch up with what I may have missed. We toured the South Bank site and chatted about generalities while driving around Belgravia, but never came to sketching. Instead, he kept evading, diverted onto explaining a Country-House plan by Robert Smythson (or was it Edwin Lutyens?).

Sometimes I wonder what would have happened, if instead of leaving university in 1968 to work for Stirling, I had joined the "Texas Rangers" at Cornell. It would surely have short-circuited my Frankfurt School tribulations and possibly gotten me where I wanted to be a little earlier. Although, in retrospect, Adorno meeting Rowe is not an unattractive prospect, their supreme mastery of speech would have made them a formidable duo. Class struggle and chamber music, Colin's flirtation with oppositional terminology without ever committing, was also a recurring pastime of

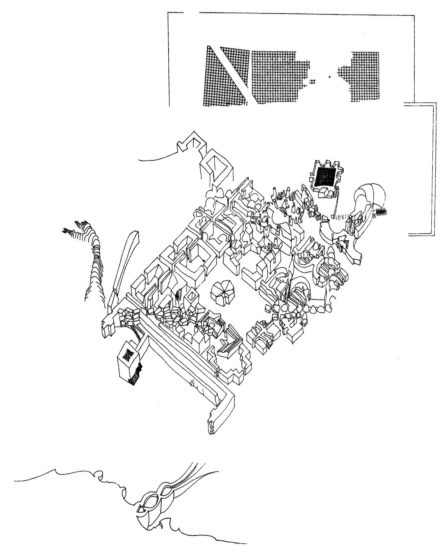

FIGURE 21 Rainer Jagals, Cityspace Fantasy/Vision (1967)

Credit: Courtesy Galerie Strecker, Rainer Jagals, exhibit catalogue, Dezember 1967–Februar 1968, Berlin

critical theory. Indeed, why "program" and "typology," "Versailles and Wiesbaden," or "literal" and "phenomenal" transparency had to be presented as forever irreconcilable opposites is left unexplained. Rowe never offers possible resolutions, not even through his promotion of Rainer Jagals's lightweight sketches, which he so admired. One had to wait for another generation before one could get real, synthetic theories. Theodor W. and Colin were both resistant to apodictic stances for fear of ever more tragic error. As a consequence, they both indulged in avoidances, hinting at possibilities and potentials rather than drawing or describing them. Critical thinking absorbed so much of their energy that they were unable to transcend it. Their aesthetic of fragments did not engender the new "new world" they so ardently pursued. And yet, Colin would not be satisfied with the Cornell studio projects nor would Adorno find fulfillment in a purely serial musical world. And that is due to the fact that literary criticism can be no more literature than architectural criticism can be architecture. It may bring down walls but it will not build the new house or the new

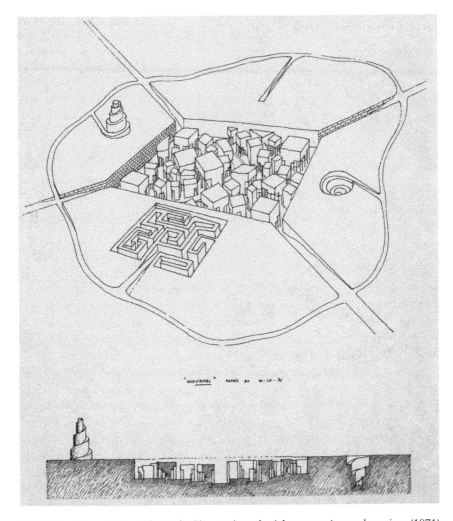

FIGURE 22 Léon Krier, Labyrinth City, project. Aerial perspective and section (1971). Ink with gouache on paper, 11 5/8 × 8 1/4 in. Gift of The Howard Gilman Foundation. (12.13.2000) The Museum of Modern Art, New York, NY, USA.

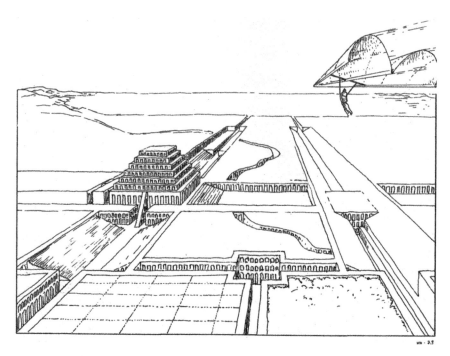

FIGURE 23 Léon Krier, Untitled (1973)

Credit: © Léon Krier

city, let alone a new country or continent. For all their declared dread of the "brave new world," they both never lost faith in all-redeeming "newness." For instance, Colin feared that a wave of rationalism would kill "the possibility of intrinsic novelty." As if novelty and newness were avoidable and as if anything could ever be the same. In his own words, "newness continually occurs within the world . . . (too often like the corks of cheap champagne bottles popping) . . ."

I haven't read *Collage City* to this day, not for lack of trying. I quite simply do not get the idea. It is an art historian's game. It is too much of a box of polished antiques, a diversion from the central themes of architecture and urbanism. It confuses architectural project and urban master planning. The first is to do with the design of buildings, and the second, with designing development lots and codes which regulate the design of buildings individually and in concert. But what *Collage City* promotes instead is a vast single design object even if paradoxically composed as an assemblage of set pieces chosen from a collection of luminous precedents. It confuses what Quatremère de Quincy had so definitively cleared, notably the difference between "type" and "model." Similarly I never understood why Jagals's doodles were championed by Colin as the panacea, as the global, all-surpassing synthetic vision wrought in agony by a supreme artist from the claws of death.

I only recently discovered that I knew much less of Colin Rowe than I should have. Indeed, there was a lot of unfinished business not just between him and myself, but with his followers as well. Having only just read Rowe's collection of essays in *As I Was Saying*, I am puzzled and almost angered by the fact that he never developed a synthetic vision of his ideas. Why he did not turn these ideas into a major American and worldwide movement—like CIAM before him or New Urbanism now? By the late 1960s, he had certainly assembled enough ideas, talent, and gray matter around him and held the moral and intellectual eminence to bring all this together. His career reminds me somewhat of the athlete who refuses to cross the finish line and pick up the trophy; or was he the priest, who having lost his faith, couldn't lay off the garment?

In 1954 Rowe had declared the intention to "neither revive the Beaux-Arts nor to erect a new Bauhaus, but [. . .] that from the remnants of both [. . .] by a process of trial and error something of significance might be constructed."[2] Over the years, exactly by trial and error, and often working through his many assistants, he, like so many other neo-traditional architects and urbanists, integrated ideas from much further afield into his practice. This culminated in the 1980s with studio projects in Providence, Rome, or Pitigliano, where all traces of architectural or urbanistic modernism, even of *Collage City*, are serenely absent. Paradoxically, he didn't accompany these radical steps and schemes with parallel theoretical underpinnings; what is evident, however, is that industrial redundancies like modular mega-structures and modernist icons, which so characterized the Cornell studios of the 1960s and 1970s, are silently left behind, abandoned without a trace.

These at once discrete and revolutionary changes of mind in his retirement years notwithstanding, I have to conclude that despite his many declarations of independence, Colin remained married to the modernist agenda. He feared that to subscribe once and for all to the idea of reconstruction, typology, and tradition were steps he was personally unable to take even though he permitted, encouraged, and applauded

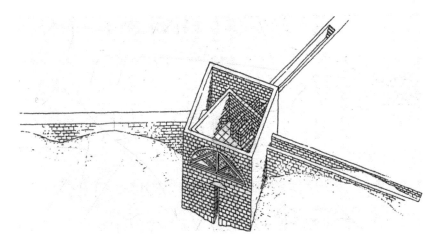

FIGURE 24 Léon Krier, From L.K. To C.R. (1975)

Credit: © Léon Krier

younger people for doing so: this included me. Despite affirmations to the contrary, his mind was more profoundly marked by art history than by the art and *métier* of building and planning. He was also more enamored by idea of epochal change than of incremental improvement, more of revolution than evolution.

Did Colin experience a conversion toward the end of his career? I don't believe he did, but nor did he have to. Traditional architecture, unlike modernism, is not a religion, and unlike religion it does not demand that you believe in the unprovable or to suspend judgment in the face of factual and aesthetic evidence. It allows you to appreciate works of art of any origin or ideology without joining the party or clouding your judgment, and hence to enjoy modernist masterpieces while refusing to practice that particular *maniera*. The explanation is simple; while modernism is founded on the rejection of traditional architecture, the latter is an integrative theoretical and practical discipline. Traditional architecture integrates into its practice those ideas and techniques which withstand the test of time, of technical, aesthetic, and moral judgments. If modernism produces ideas of aesthetic and practical value, these will be seamlessly integrated into the vast body and vocabularies of traditional architectures and technology. Without declaring it necessarily as a goal, Rowe has left us with the living example how to do just that.

Notes

1   David Watkin, *Thomas Hope 1769–1831 and the Neo-Classical Idea* (London: John Murray, 1968).
2   Colin Rowe, *As I Was Saying: Recollections and Miscellaneous Essays*, vol. 1, ed. Alexander Caragonne (Cambridge, MA: MIT Press, 1996), 50.

"It was clear that Rowe was an incredible amateur in terms of somebody who loves things, an amateur of those moments where systems fall apart or achieve the ends of their logic and transform into something else. . . . The irony for me was that seemed something fundamentally not accessible to any designer, because you could *be* the system, but you could never be its bankruptcy or its fiasco. . . . that's also why I became interested in him. Rowe's sentence 'You can enjoy utopian aesthetics without suffering the embarrassment of utopian politics' is the key to Rowe. In the 1970s, politics were still much more present than today, so that was a particularly obscene definition in my eyes."

BEING O.M.U.'S GHOSTWRITER

*Rem Koolhaas
in conversation with Robert Somol[1]*

> *What we have here is not so much a structure as an icon, . . . a discipline by means of which an invertebrate expressionism can be reduced to the appearance of reason.*
> —Colin Rowe, on Dom-ino

> *Limp, unprovable conjectures . . . supported (made critical) by the crutches of Cartesian rationality.*
> —Rem Koolhaas, on paranoid-critical method

I first have to confess a certain anxiety about broaching the topic of Colin Rowe with you as I've entertained a long-standing conspiracy theory about the relationship of your work to his, especially the influence of Rowe's contextualism on your ideas about the city. So I'm not sure what's worse: if you deny the connection, the thesis loses its plausibility, but if you confirm it, the quality of surprise is lost. The only thing worse would be letting someone else ask these questions. So here we are. There seem to have been several possible institutional intersections between you and Rowe: at the Architectural Association (AA) in London, Cornell University, the Institute for Architecture and Urban Studies in New York. When did you first encounter the Rowe effect, and what were your impressions? Were the zones of influence present at the AA as a student?

I don't think I ever met Rowe at the AA directly, but the Rowe effect was very strong because there was Sam (Thomas) Stevens and Jim Stirling. Stevens was a friend of Rowe's from Liverpool where they had studied together; I think that a large part of what Rowe thought, and some of the brilliance of the "Transparency" essays, were things that had been elaborated together with Sam Stevens. Stevens was the dominant intellectual idiot savant type in the school, who could hold forth on almost anything in the most unbelievably brilliant way; he was absolutely incredible. He had a stunning erudition that went from everything modern to everything baroque and back. I could do some research about the extent to which they were really twinned or had common histories, but as far as I remember, I think that they had a very overlapping history roughly until Rowe went to America. He was also engaged in transforming an English house in Hempstead into a Corbusian house with incredible drawings that I still remember.

I recall reading somewhere that there were rumors about a Rowe bid to assume the directorship of the school before Alvin Boyarsky?

I don't think so, and I was involved in that revolution. We got rid of the director and had a search, but as far as I know the only other serious candidate was Kenneth Frampton, not Rowe.

I didn't realize Boyarsky wasn't already established when you arrived there.

No, when I went Michael Lloyd was principal. Two years into being a student there was a huge scandal because it turned out that he was the leader of a religious sect in the school that would occasionally tap certain people on the back and say, "Okay, you may be one of the chosen." It was really a big deal because the students would disappear somewhere into the countryside to live in colonies. At some point there was an explosion because one of the sect's theses is that there is only a certain amount of knowledge, and therefore, it doesn't make sense to share it with everyone; it's only for the chosen. That seemed to be the wrong concept for a school. So we got rid of him. But it was slightly flawed because at some point you didn't know who was part of it. For instance, there were strong rumors that Peter Cook was part of it also. And maybe he was.

So then we, a group of staff and students, organized a search. It is possible that Rowe was a candidate, but I don't remember it, and in any case not a serious candidate. Ken was a serious candidate. Many people were eager to have him. He flew to London the night before his interview, so he arrived ashen-faced. The first thing he said is "From now on we're going to work on standardized format," and this was in 1970 or something. And he was incredibly serious that everyone was going to work on A4s so that there would be uniformity. But he lost.

The first time I heard Boyarsky, he was giving a lecture on Chicago, and it was an unbelievable lecture. Really, it was sulfurous, it was so dangerous. He was raising the notion of city to a dangerous level. So at that point I had an enormous sympathy for him. It's later at the AA that he became more arty and more poetic. That was partly under the influence of Dalibor Veseley. But I don't know if he had any sympathy for Rowe.

The fifth year at the AA was under the control of Cook. And Cook really hated me from the first moment I was in the school. It was really a problem. Three months into the school he called me the "boring fascist." He took me apart and said there were schools that were more suitable to my work and that he would help me get in there. After that I found a home in a unit that was run by Elia Zenghelis, an old partner of Ken. So that was a kind of access of the hardcore modernist. Since it was so clear that I would have a horrible time with Cook—the knives were out—I applied for a Harkness Fellowship and got that. So I didn't graduate from the AA, except that Alvin gave me a diploma a year later since I had done a kind of thesis project, the "Berlin Wall as Architecture."

And then you went to study at Cornell. What attracted you to study with O. Mathias Ungers?

FIGURE 25   Rem Koolhaas, from "Berlin Wall as Architecture" photo series (ca. 1971)
Credit: © Alfred Ziethen Verlag; Courtesy OMA; Office for Metropolitan Architecture

I went to Cornell because when I worked on the Berlin Wall I had discovered all the publications Ungers produced about his seminar when he was a professor in Berlin. The seminar was unbelievably impressive where he took issues—like "highways and buildings" or "parks and buildings"—always located in Berlin; for this purpose, the city was contained like a petri dish, and he made an inventory that went from the somewhat literal to huge housing projects to utopian mega-structures for Berlin. The results of that seminar were published in a very straightforward manner, but with very beautiful drawings. He also had some really miraculous students who made interesting amalgamations, because it was clear that Ungers was at first

FIGURE 26 Alfred Ziethen Verlag postcard of Berlin from Rem Koolhaas's "Berlin Wall as Architecture" photo series (ca. 1971)

Credit: © Alfred Ziethen Verlag; Courtesy OMA; Office for Metropolitan Architecture

a hardcore modernist, and then gravitated toward Team X. But he remained on the fringes of Team X: there was always a kind of hesitation whether a German could actually be sensitive enough to urban conditions. He had a huge formal ingenuity and an incredible knowledge of historical sources. One of the things I remember very well is, for instance, the way he took all the formal ingredients of Berlin and had one student develop a project that was a super-thin, super-monumental slab. So Ungers was one of the first people who started to develop modernism inflected by historical figures, such as Schinkel and others. But not in a postmodern way; it had deeper relationships. Ungers also had a seminar on Schinkel that was truly astonishing because it really opened up all the procedures and all the concepts. When I was in Berlin studying the Wall, I found this file of books that fascinated me to the point that I haunted him in Ithaca.

The story is that Rowe was a supporter of Ungers before he became the chair at Cornell, and that in fact he helped him get the appointment, but that when Rowe returned in 1970 there was a major falling out. What was your sense of the ideological faultiness at Cornell?

It was never explained in detail, but Ungers always felt that the moment he stepped off the boat, he stepped into a hostile situation. I think Rowe found some of the last things that Ungers had been doing kind of shapeless and, furthermore, systematic investigations of randomness and chance—as for example what he had done for the competition for the Parliament in Bonn. It was a kind of democratic, shifting, cellular, and vaguely mega-structural project. For Rowe that was a reason to denigrate him and find him a figure of ridicule exactly at the moment he arrived.

Because he had a very strange character, Ungers could only generate intelligence by doing something. He could not have an a priori opinion or analysis, it was only by becoming the thing that he finally realized what it was.

So the opposite of Rowe in some way?

Yes, the opposite. That's why he was so physically engaged with the particular. He had a weekly seminar and it was almost orgasmic, so deeply exciting. I never had a teaching like that before or since. Just the beauty of his ideas and the beauty of what he showed, endless variations of certain things. What he was interested in with Schinkel was how a single idea would transform in an endless chain of iterations. That was what we would do, too. And I think that was already too abstract for Rowe.

How would Ungers project these variations?

For instance, it could be in the typologies of housing or in a single block that morphs into a little village without almost any pressure coming from the context. That was the other interesting thing. I still had some connections with Team X, so at some point Ungers organized a Team X seminar at Cornell where he got some people from Team X to visit. One of Ungers's stories is that Bakema came from the plane saying, "I want to give a lecture, where is the lecture," and immediately started giving lectures. The next morning Bakema came to Ungers's house, stumbled to the bedroom, took the blankets, pulled them up, and took Ungers by the legs and shook him awake, saying, "I want to talk about Architecture!" in a form of architectural violence. Then when they were sitting around the breakfast table, Bakema was making a point so strongly that Ungers fell on the ground. Ungers was telling this story with total indignation, and I said, "Don't you see that this is your method? That by letting yourself be overwhelmed by an apparently larger force you generate your own aesthetic and your own understanding?"

Ungers was very lonely and he was also in a crisis. That project in Bonn marked a crisis because he gave up his more formal predilections and began to think about more systematic things. I started to work with him, and we did a series of competitions together. It was a really interesting experience because it was the only time that I worked for somebody else, and I realized how wonderful it was to be somebody's ghostwriter: I could be a better Ungers than Ungers himself at that point. But in a way that got him in a mood of real confidence, and that probably angered Rowe even more. There were notorious stories of snowball fights. Basically, at some point the two clusters were saying you have to get together, and at some point Rowe came at Christmas Eve, and then the Ungers's children threw snowballs and he retreated. It's really too childish for words.

The result was that I spent only one evening with Rowe in my entire life. That was before I started at Cornell on a kind of fact-finding mission to see where I wanted to go. He received me at his house with an incredibly eloquent and endless flow of anecdotes, books on your lap, the whole works. It was vaguely familiar from

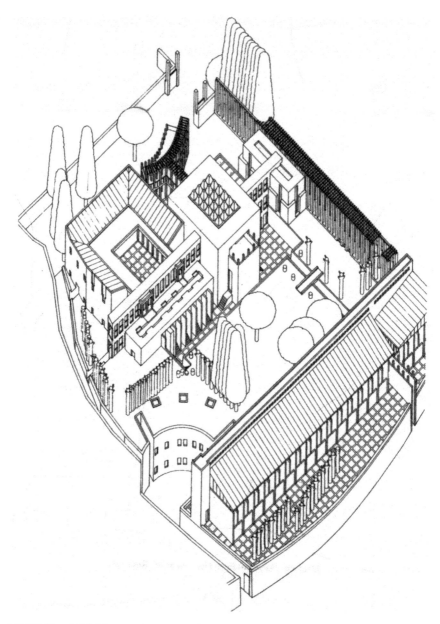

FIGURE 27 O.M. Ungers, German Embassy to the Vatican in Rome, competition project axon (1965)

Credit: Courtesy of Ungers Archiv für Architekturwissenschaften UAA, Cologne

Sam Stevens, so I knew the language, the incredibly outlandish formulations, and the self-evident ironic arrogance of how they pose their arguments. But because I was connected to Ungers, there was never a chance of seeing him seriously again.

You heard the tone of ironic arrogance that you knew from Sam Stevens?

It was very familiar. Stirling, Rowe, and Stevens had been together in Liverpool, so that's where they generated the early iteration of an English modernity. I think that was very much a creation of the industrial north. In comparison, Peter Smithson was effete. And although sometimes Stirling had resonances with Team X, I don't think he ever attended a meeting.

I only saw Rowe from the outside, and from the outside he presented an impressive spectacle, an impressive knowledge. The only thing that was vaguely suspicious was the nature of his acolytes. The way they were almost like goons.

Did you find yourself developing another voice against the ironic arrogance?

I don't think it was strong enough to me to elicit a response, and it was so incredibly crafted; it's not something you felt you could do a lot with.

So my real understanding was considerably enlarged at the Institute for Architecture and Urban Studies (IAUS), simply by Peter Eisenman and his anecdotes about Rowe. Peter exaggerated it completely, always suggesting that it was only by traveling with Rowe, and kind of sleeping with Rowe, that being exposed to a complete and relentless overdose that he became who he was. But that is what I saw as the influence of Rowe on Peter: that he had locked up somebody completely in the prison of architecture and thrown away the key. That is an unbroken line from Peter to Greg Lynn that continues that whole thing. Maybe it is the French tendency combined with architecture that formed my orientation.

So it's true that Rowe was very present—both in Peter's stories and in his occasional presence at the Institute. And of course, by not having any intimacy with him, it was very possible to have an intellectual attitude toward him.

And in contrast to those other acolytes that were the marines, how did Peter escape?

I think Rowe had different moments. For instance, the Stirling moment was a moment of intense common creativity, because I'm sure that he dared exciting work, to make it possible to be modern in England—because before that it wasn't possible. The funny thing is that Stirling was an incredibly nice man, and although I was a nobody, he was always incredibly nice to me and supported me—for instance he wrote recommendations for my Harkness Fellowship. Once he was staying with Richard Meier and he let me see Meier's apartment when he was absent, and there was a collective gloating about how horrible it was.

What was beautiful about Stirling is that you could never understand whether what he did was intelligent or was really almost stupid backed with an incredible willpower, or whether it was a gift or something that was incredibly forced that in the end yielded something. That was never quite clear. That made it interesting because you were always thinking, "What the hell is going on here?" and "Where does that come from?" He was a really intriguing and important presence at that point, and so I was confronted with how impressive and creative Rowe must have been through Stirling. Stirling and Ungers were friendly, so Stirling was definitely not in a camp. Then I met Peter. In Peter's case it was his mentality and erudition that had the effect much more than any effect on the work, so that also looked impressive.

It was clear that Rowe was an incredible amateur in terms of somebody who loves things, an amateur of those moments where systems fall apart or achieve the ends of their logic and transform into something else. That was the key to his whole system of thrills. The irony for me was that seemed something fundamentally not accessible to any designer, because you could *be* the system, but you could never be its bankruptcy or its fiasco. Yet all his work was based on incorporating, finding, arguing, and extracting from the context those clues that could then enable you to design the shack.

And Peter would also focus on those moments . . .

I think Peter made only those moments in a certain way.

Like Cornell, the IAUS was another institution colored in some ways by the influence of Rowe. To what degree did your research at the institute connect with or remain independent from Peter's larger project and his struggle within and against the Rowe legacy? It seems your work was quite independent from his, and colored by an encounter with Foucault, who was also at Cornell when you were.

In London I started to read Roland Barthes, and Barthes was an incredibly important influence. Another equally important influence was Charles Jencks. But he was important simply because he never ever liked anything I did. He was relentless about it. But I'm incredibly grateful, because he was giving me the freshest critique of postmodernism as a constant earphone—how bad I was, how I couldn't do doors, how I didn't know what entrances were, and so on—and it never changed. But in a way it was a very generous thing for him to do.

The year I went to Ithaca, Charles visited us at our house. We would occasionally go to the streets at dusk, shuffling out, him in his blue Beatles glasses. On one of these walks I saw a couple drive by arguing among themselves whether he was Charles or not, and that was Hubert Damisch and his wife—an American who was the niece of Zelevsky who was a professor at Harvard and the right-hand man of Josep Lluís Sert and therefore important in Jencks's life. So basically he introduced us to the Damischs and we became friends. The first time we had dinner, she used the opportunity to tell her husband that she was pregnant—her husband didn't want any children—and so she said, "Oh, by the way, I'm pregnant." But because we were there, he couldn't say anything. And she turned out to be already six months' pregnant. Then they went to a faculty party for Christmas and found a feminist who said, "Oh, pregnancy is nonsense; you don't have to be nine months' pregnant; you can just have the child." She had the child the same evening. So in Hubert's consciousness his wife was pregnant for only one month. But anyway, he knew Foucault, and we became friends with Foucault, and went to that seminar. So that was important. When he went back to Paris he also introduced me to Barthes. So for me *Delirious New York* is a French book written in English.

Jenck's postmodernism was not as fully developed in 1972 as it would become, but was that something you could already contend with?

No, it was really *Meaning in Architecture*, which was a more interesting and inspiring moment. I wrote *Delirous New York* in 1976 when I was back in London, so I was only doing research in America. But the work I was doing at the Institute was really to find an answer to Jencks, not to be sympathetic to Peter. So for me it was an attempt to address all the issues of the figurative and the historical. It was addressed to postmodernism. That was the irony because I was the only person at the Institute who was interested in that—the rest of the Institute was a kind of fortress of rejection for everyone from Robert Venturi to Jencks. I took it incredibly seriously, and almost without liking it. So, for instance, I left out those drawings in *Delirious New York* in the second edition. But I think it was worth doing, and I definitely took it very seriously.

Although coming from different sources and addressed to different audiences, you and Peter were both working on the issue of how to give modernism a contemporary force. For Peter, the problem was explicitly with Rowe in that Rowe institutionalized modernism by classicizing it. And so Peter turns to recuperating a new Le Corbusier, first through a structuralist reading of Corb's Dom-ino diagram. Your work also reinvigorates modernism, but by grafting it to metropolitan and mass cultural artifacts, to the empirical and fictional data of America. So your found "cartoon theorem" against Rowe's explicit denigration of the American frame, and maybe also against Peter's implicit continuity of that dismissal by his need to look to high European practice. Meanwhile, you were embracing specifically the American situation.

Of course, that was the whole irony. There was a double anathema to what I was doing. On one hand, it was American, and everyone was united in the certainty that America could never produce anything serious. It was also about surrealism, against which there was an equal coalition of resistance. In that case it extended to Rosalind Krauss, who also became a part of the picture, first as Ken's girlfriend. So even though she was clearly intrigued, she at least talked to me, because the rest would never really talk to us. They were very friendly as human beings, but the work was out of the picture. Only in the mid- to late 1990s has surrealism finally gotten through to them in the guise of the formless. So for them it was an impossible thing to take seriously. Rowe was also completely revolted by surrealism . . . by the mediocrity of surrealism.

But you have said yourself that you were not necessarily interested in its formal proposals . . .
No, no, but in its writings and method.

Although never explicitly invoked by you (except, perhaps, in the transformation of Rowe's "Blenheim of the Welfare State" to your own "Las Vegas of the Welfare State"), there has always seemed to be a secret correspondence—collision, confrontation, complicity—between your work and Rowe's. At the AA, the field trip to study the Berlin Wall was juxtaposed to the measuring of Palladian villas in Southern Europe. Delirious New York and "Typical Plan" serve as inversions or systematic dismantling of Rowe's priorities in the "Transparency" and "Chicago Frame" essays, for example, the shift from Rowe's "shallow space" to your "deep plan," or the articulation of figure-ground to your "apotheosis of background." Even Rowe's denigrated sketch "Program without Plan" (a tuning fork with blobs) resembles your endorsement of Dali's paranoid-critical method, while your verbal description of that surrealist procedure perversely echoes Rowe's discussion of the Domino diagram. How conscious were these repetitions and deviations or how useful were they in advancing the work? Did you have any direct engagements with the transparency essays?

You know, I did not. I started looking at the Texas essays but I just couldn't—I really tried, but I was so convinced that the reading was a complete fabrication—I don't know exactly why. So it was really only with *Collage City* that I started reading the work closely, strangely enough. But it was at least about the city, and so had some connection.

In Collage City, *Rowe grades Corb a good architect, but a bad urbanist. In* Delirious New York, *you reveal Corb's Paris plan, perversely, as a form of collage despite Rowe, or as a game of exquisite corpse—so a collage perhaps more Breton than Picasso. Between your "fuck context" and "future context," you similarly undermine and extend the limited Cornell understanding of contextualism (of past or present). How much of your urban thinking is a response to* Collage City?

In that case, I was aware of it all, so that was deliberate. It's certainly true that my relationship to contextualism was deeply influenced by Rowe, and by the luxury of the exposure to contextualism in all its possible dimensions. It made me very deliberate in terms of where I did not want to go and trying to invent a contextualism that was plausible. That was very true.

At least as interesting as the divergences are the zones of overlap between you and Rowe. Both of you link questions of form and politics, and this may account for your respective investments in the urban, for the city is in the first instance a form that politics takes. This sense of the link between form and politics appears lost on both of your followers. But there is a politics to Rowe . . .

Absolutely, and that's also why I became interested in him. Rowe's sentence "You can enjoy utopian aesthetics without suffering the embarrassment of utopian politics" is the key to Rowe. In the 1970s, politics were still much more present than today, so that was a particularly obscene definition in my eyes. Even though by the 1990s it was not really possible to be political in the system. Only now is it becoming possible to repoliticize. In a way I was fundamentally wrong-footed: I was not that kind of liberal, but at the same time I did not have a platform, and for the time being no platform was available, where you could actually define a political action.

To what extent is form linked to, or necessary for, a political ambition?

Maybe not form, but the accumulation of form, which is the city. For me it has been very exciting that Toni Negri has read *Delirious New York*, and now the *Harvard Guide to Shopping* and the *Great Leap Forward*, as deeply political books.

But you have no idea of how completely alien I felt when I came from the Continent to England. I felt that I was in a totally alien culture, because by that time I had been influenced by Italian movies, Antonioni, Fluxus, and that streak of modernity. It was weird to be confronted by hippies and Celtic issues. So for me it was a Celtic world to which I went, which resisted all speculation. It was also exciting to be there exactly because it was so inarticulate. I learned a lot by being in some kind of fairy tale: If you listened to people like Peter Smithson, it was so bizarre; there was absolutely no argument, there was just feeling and emotion.

Probably Rowe would be equally dismissive of that culture of irrationality and demand more of an intellectual structure . . .

Yes, but he was the other extreme of the Anglo-Saxon spectrum, with a hatred of speculation. The others evidenced simply an absence thereof, so from absence to hatred. In that sense it was strange to come to America and to feel more speculative activity and more intellectualism here.

Note

1   This conversation was initially recorded in Los Angeles, California, in May 2002.

Transparency, Collage, Montage

"The similarities between Giedion's and Rowe's writings may not be their most striking feature, but they are arresting enough for us to wonder why, on the evidence of these particular examples [of Le Corbusier's buildings], the two historians should so often be presented as occupying opposing ideological positions."

TRANSPARENCY REVISITED

Alan Colquhoun

These notes discuss what I take to be the most contested aspect of Rowe and Slutzky's essay of 1963 titled "Transparency, Literal and Phenomenal": the close relation it posits between modern architecture and cubist painting, using Le Corbusier's Villa at Garches as a paradigm. In order to be able to approach this famous essay from a slightly new perspective, I compare it to Sigfried Giedion's first book *Building in France: Building in Iron, Building in Ferroconcrete* at the end of which the author makes somewhat similar claims for Le Corbusier's housing at Pessac. It would be useful, however, to preface this discussion with a few words about the 19th-century formalist tradition, without which both Rowe and Slutzky's and Giedion's ideas would have been inconceivable.

Very soon after the emergence of the modern system of the Fine Arts—comprising poetry, music, painting, sculpture, and architecture—in the second half of the 18th century, both philosophers of art and artists began to speculate on the implications of art's new-won freedom from social dependence, especially as it concerned the classical concept of *mimèsis*. One of its main implications was that the work of art should be perceived as having its own density or opacity, and as being connected to the "real" world only through the mediation of both the subjectivity of the artist and the materiality of each art—words, tones, visual representations in the round and on the flat surface, and so on. The "meaning" of the work of art was perceived as lying on the surface of the work itself and as differing from the meaning of the referent, to which it had previously been tied through verbal conventions and universal ideas (*ut pictura poesis*). Art was no longer a supplement to discursive knowledge, but a form of knowledge in its own right. This opacity of art was stressed, not only by philosophers like Conrad Fiedler or historians like Alois Riegl and Heinrich Wölfflin but by artists as well. For Richard Wagner, the impressions of life, however powerful, were nothing but catalysts for the artist's inner vision: "The artistic structure . . . appears in no sense the result of, but, on the contrary, a liberation from these vital impressions."[1] For

Stephane Mallarmé, "[t]here is a modern tendency to think of the world as, on the one hand, immediate and natural, and, on the other, essential. This changes human thought and silently puts into circulation a coin of universal reportage, in which all the genres of writing participate, except that of literature . . . How wonderful to transform a fact of nature and make it almost disappear within the play of the word."[2]

Although this new concept of art was fundamental to "avant-garde" art in general, there were obvious problems in applying it to architecture. Throughout modern history there has been uncertainty as to whether architecture should be described as a "mechanical" or a "liberal" art. In the 16th century, architecture became one of the three arts based on "*disegno*" and thus one of the liberal arts. In the Enlightenment it became one of the "fine arts," but for Kant, and later Schopenhauer, it was a "dependent" art due to its purposive function and the ambiguous figure of the frame. While, in the other arts, the turn toward technique and materiality led to a reflexivity in which content was indissolubly linked to form—the work of art becoming, figuratively and often literally, its own content—in architecture the reverse process took place and technique (structure and materials) became associated with the work's practical purpose. To focus on architecture's material conditions meant to focus on the world outside architecture. But the idea that there was an irreducible formal side of architecture returned, alongside the "facticity" of the *Neue Sachlichkeit*, when, partly due to the disappearance of handicraft and rapid development of mechanization, notions such as Gestalt, the Zeitgeist and the *Kunstwollen* became prominent in architectural discourse, giving priority to "form" over material and craftsmanship and inaugurating an awkward alliance between materialism and idealism.

The idea of the opacity of art, and, by extension, of architecture, is never very far from the surface of Rowe and Slutzky's "Transparency" essay, although it is never actually mentioned. What appears to be suggested is that transparency as applied to art in general in a metaphorical sense can be applied to architecture in particular in a literal sense. The curtain wall of Gropius's Bauhaus building is presented as bearing the same relation to function ("purposiveness," in Kantian terms) as naturalist painting has to the world as given to the senses (a window onto reality). But because architecture exists in the real three-dimensional world whether it is opaque or transparent, it would have to qualify, in its own essence, as a naturalistic art, which would be absurd. This however leaves untouched the phenomenal difference (and therefore the aesthetic difference) between solid walls and glass, which is one of the valid concerns of Rowe and Slutzky. What they are saying is that Le Corbusier, unlike Gropius, treats the opaque skin of his buildings in such a way as to suggest the frame structure that they both conceal and reveal. Conversely (but this is not mentioned by Rowe and Slutzky) when Le Corbusier uses a curtain wall (as in the Armée de Salut building) it is different from the curtain wall of the Bauhaus in that, in spite of its transparency (which had important but different connotations for Le Corbusier), its tautness and the detailing of the mullions gives it a certain opacity.

The essay opens with a discussion of cubist painting and with a long citation from Gyorgy Kepes: "If one sees two or more figures overlapping one another and each of them claims the common overlapping part, then one is confronted with a

FIGURE 28   Walter Gropius, Bauhaus, Dessau (1925–26)

Credit: © Burçin Yildirim

contradiction of spatial dimensions. To resolve this contradiction one must assume a new optical quality. The figures are endowed with transparency: that is to say they are able to inter-penetrate without the optical destruction of each other. Transparency, however, implies more than an optical characteristic, it implies . . . the simultaneous perception of different spatial locations. Space not only recedes but fluctuates in a continuous activity . . . one sees each figure now as the closer now as the further one."

This quotation is the key reference for Rowe and Slutzky's whole thesis. But they modify Kepes in one respect, claiming that his definition of "transparency" implies that it can be interpreted in two different senses—a literal (rational) and a phenomenal (felt) sense. In literal transparency, figures are realistically represented as consisting of a translucent material such as glass. An unproblematic, pre-cubist figure/ground hierarchy is represented and the objects float in an illusionistic void. In phenomenal transparency, figures are represented as semi-opaque and the hidden part of a recessive object is suggested rather than stated. The objects exist in shallow, non-perspectival space, within a matrix in which the figure / ground relation is constantly fluctuating. "With Picasso, Braque, Léger, Ozenfant [and Mondrian], we are never conscious of the picture plane functioning in any passive role . . . both it . . . and the objects placed upon it . . . are endowed with an equal capacity to stimulate."[3] The two types of transparency are illustrated by paintings by Moholy Nagy and Fernand Léger, respectively.

When they come to apply this theory to architecture, Rowe and Slutzky admit that "inevitable confusions arise. For while painting can only imply a third dimension, architecture cannot suppress it." However, they do not conclude from this that the concept of phenomenal transparency cannot be applied to architecture but simply that it will "be more difficult to achieve." To show that it *can* be achieved, they carry out two detailed analyses of Le Corbusier's villa Stein de Monzie at Garches—one of the garden façade, the other of the principal floor.

The garden facade of Garches, Rowe and Slutzky suggest, stimulates the observer to try to understand its internal spatial "structure." This structure is described as a series of imaginary vertical planes, parallel to the facade, coinciding with the structural grid, and implied on the outside by a number of fragmentary visual clues (the back wall of the terrace, the set back roof structures, the flank wall of the terrace, the recessed structural plane of the ground floor). As Rowe and Slutzky summarize it, "[i]n itself, each of these planes is incomplete ... Yet it is with these parallel planes as points of reference that the facade is organized, and the implication of all is that of a vertical layer-like stratification of the interior space of the building, of a succession of laterally extended spaces traveling one behind the other."

The discussion of the interior focuses on the problem of the central reception room. This room runs from front to back of the house and, the authors say, contradicts the strong lateral layering of the floor as a whole. This space is, however, affected by a series of fragmentary plastic events—the lateral main stair, the piano shaped balcony, the convex parabolic screen to the dining room, the back wall of the terrace, and the "slot of space" behind the facades—all of which tend to reinforce the lateral stratification of the space without totally suppressing the counter-thrust of the central living space. Two readings of space overlap without destroying each other. This ambiguity is made possible (though this is not mentioned in the text) by the use of a structural grid which, relieving the partitions of any structural function, converts them into discontinuous planes, to be positioned and shaped at will. We are therefore in the presence of two variables, with all the possibilities of simultaneous interpretation that this implies.

These analyses give rise to several reservations. First, Rowe and Slutzky do not succeed in showing the close analogy between painting and architecture that they imply exists. That there is an analogy would be foolish to deny, but the essay leaves it tantalizingly vague and does not draw attention to the ways in which the perception of a painting and a building differ. In the Léger painting, for example, the receding planes are generated from the two-dimensional surface and remain palpably attached to the flat plane of the picture. Recession is implied by relative position; the objects depicted do not diminish with distance, and there is no aerial medium separating the planes of which they are composed. The viewer, who is immobile, has an immediate and tactile experience of the various planes as they slide past and partially obscure each other. In a building, which is extended in real space, this tactile experience is relatively weak. Its effects must be accumulated in time. This is not to deny that

FIGURE 29 Le Corbusier, Villa Stein de Monzie Garches (1926–28)

Credit: © Ralitza Petit

FIGURE 30 Le Corbusier, Villa Stein de Monzie, axon (1926–28)

Credit: © F.L.C. / ADAGP, Paris / Artists Rights Society (ARS), New York 2014

planes may be positioned to have a rhyming effect from a single position. Modern architecture provides many examples of this, not only in Le Corbusier but also in De Stijl and Mies Van der Rohe, but these effects are just as likely to be seen sequentially by a mobile viewer, who has to synthesize them.

Second, Rowe and Slutzky's description seems to ascribe a sort of inevitability to the plan, ignoring its earlier incarnations. In Garches, the tripartite symmetry of the original sketch was based on an unusual programmatic requirement: the double occupancy of the house. The plan went through a number of transformations due to a change in the program—from double to single occupancy. These included the drastic migration of the huge terrace from the center of the house to its periphery.[4] None of the earlier solutions gave the strong emphasis to the lateral layering that we find in the final solution and which is the basis of Rowe and Slutzky's thesis. Throughout these changes, the ABABA rhythm of the longitudinal grid and the position of the stairs remained exactly the same. It was the separation of structure from partitions (the "free plan") that made possible the change of the plan without changing the structural grid. One of the reasons why such "accidental" facts of a building's history should not be ignored is that an analysis such as Rowe and Slutzky's, although seeking to bracket out every factor that is irrelevant to a purely formal reading, cannot avoid including aspects of plan organization that were due to programmatic requirements. These traces of accidental events of history cannot be excluded from a building plan. It can never be reduced to "pure" form. None of these facts absolutely invalidates Rowe and Slutzky's interpretation of the plan. But these facts make it less immutable and more subject to chance than they imply, diluting the essentialist tone of their argument.

Third, the exclusive importance attached to the lateral stratification of the plan seems exaggerated. Such a stratification is, of course, inherent in a cubist painting, where everything "sticks" to the picture plane. But in a building—even a building that, like Garches, is basically symmetrical and can only be approached frontally—such binding constraints are lacking and the plan develops freely in a three-dimensional field. One stratification may seem to predominate over the other, but it never exists alone. There is something perverse in treating the central living space—as Rowe and Slutzky do—as a contradiction to a supposedly normative lateral stratification, when what is supposed to be at stake is cubist double reading. It is precisely this "aberrant" longitudinal space that is the most important in the house—one that forms the spine of a chiasmus from the entrance lobby to the dining room. It is in the very nature of the free plan that the space is not determined by the structural grid.

In spite of these problems, Rowe and Slutzky are able to show that Le Corbusier, in his purist houses—and especially in Garches—discovered a new power in the opacity of the plane, played it against the transparency of the structural grid, and achieved in three-dimensional space a complexity and ambiguity somewhat analogous to that which cubism had achieved on the flat surface.

At this point, Sigfried Giedion must make his appearance. In his first book, *Building in France, Building in Iron, Building in Ferroconcrete* Giedion provides a striking comparison with Rowe and Slutzky's analysis of Garches. This is perhaps surprising, given that they cast Giedion as their principal villain, guilty of confusing the literal transparency of Gropius's Bauhaus with the phenomenal transparency of cubism and Le Corbusier.

Giedion's book is notable for its highly metaphorical and lyrical—at times rather Futurist—aesthetic interpretations. The first part of the book gives a rapid history

FIGURE 31 Cover to Sigfried Giedion's *Bauen in Frankreich* (1928)

Credit: Courtesy Klinkhardt & Biermann Verlag, München

of the use of iron in French 19th-century building in terms of its Enlightenment, capitalist, and Saint-Simonian origins. The main contribution of Saint-Simonianism is seen as the transformation of a technical reality into a utopia. The positivist orientation of the French is favorably contrasted with the idealism of Germany, "which neglected reality to pursue the emanations of pure spirit." The transparency, openness, and lightness of iron structures are seen as metaphors of modern life: "Fields overlap, walls no longer define streets, the street has been transformed into a stream of movement. Rail lines and trains, together with the railroad station, form a single whole ... there is only a great, indivisible space in which relations and interpenetrations ... reign." Life is seen as bursting the bounds of art, but at the same time, art bounces back in the form of the infinite sublime. "Life" is not "social life" as in positivism or materialism; it is subjective and transcendental. The ambiguous relation of life and art is apparent in the following quotation: "One can no longer contain, like radium in a bottle, the need to create that which is called art and explain what remains of life devoid of it."

But, although these considerations are not without importance for the themes of this essay, it is with the second part of the book (or rather the final section of the second part) that we are chiefly concerned. In this part Giedion discusses Ferro concrete construction as applied in the new housing estate at Pessac by Le Corbusier (1926). There is a noticeable difference of perspective between the treatment of the steel structures in the first part and that of the concrete buildings in the second part. But, rather surprisingly, Giedion characterizes them both in the same words. They are presented as (1) neither spatial nor plastic, (2) engendering relation and interpenetration, and (3) as transgressing the boundary between inside and outside. In his introduction to the book, Sokratis Georgiadis argues plausibly that this apparent lapse is due to the fact that Giedion's immersion in cubism and neoplasticism (he might have added Futurism) was so great that it overrode all distinctions of materiality and use. Yet Giedion's detailed discussion of both "architectures" seems, in fact, to emphasize their differences rather than their similarities.

The steel structures, as exemplified by the Eiffel Tower and the Marseille Transporter Bridge, consist of linear, transparent, and non-rectangular lattices. The observer (Giedion's camera) is placed inside them, and therefore the space seems to be limitless (Limitlessness is one of the characteristics of the sublime according to Burke and Kant). The "ferro concrete" houses at Pessac, in contrast, are rectangular, opaque, planar, and non-corporeal. They are—at any rate in their initial conceptualization—discrete "objects" seen from the outside, though these objects themselves are partially opened up. This contrast is amply demonstrated by the admirable photographs used by Giedion.

Giedion, like Rowe and Slutzky, sees Le Corbusier's buildings of the 1920s as derived from his Purist paintings, an example of which he illustrates. Giedion describes this painting as representing "floating, transparent objects whose contours flow weightlessly into each other." But since these objects are in fact opaque, or at least have some opaque properties, unlike for example those in Moholy Nagy's painting, he must be using the word *transparent* in a free and metaphorical sense—in a sense that seems to have some affiliations with Rowe and Slutzky's "phenomenal."

Giedion says that the houses appear visually as ferro concrete, but his own analysis disproves this. In these houses, ferro concrete is only used in the frame, and the frame is usually suppressed, only being allowed to emerge in special conditions—for example, in the *pilotis* and the terraces. Otherwise, the structure is filled in with concrete block and is concealed by the plastered wall surface. They are materially ambiguous, and in fact they appear as planes. They are, as Giedion says, paper-thin. Their immateriality is accentuated by the fact that two differently colored surfaces often meet at right angles. When seen frontally, the house-type consisting of small row houses consists of successive parallel planes in contrasting colors that slide past each other in parallax. These and similar visual effects are the subject of Gideon's verbal "camera." One important passage in his description deserves extensive quotation:

> The flat contours of Passaic merge with the sky; the suspended canopies over the roof garden form the transition. The interplay of the units can be judged neither spatially nor plastically. Only relations count. Relation of smooth surfaces to perforated ones, relation of mass to void. Colors serve to lighten the volumes, to make surfaces advance and recede . . . These houses that so rigorously respect the planar surface are themselves penetrated with expansive, onrushing cubes of air . . . The row houses as a whole . . . reach into the space next to and behind them. Still photography does not capture them clearly . . . does one really think that the wall on the right, as taut as a movie screen and altogether deprived of its corporeality . . . [is] unrelated to the opening and the surface of the brown elements next to it? . . . the result evolves by itself from the elements of an architecture that—freed from the play of load and support—has cast off anthropomorphic shackles. We owe it to the Dutch . . . that our eyes have been opened to the oscillating relations that may arise from surfaces, lines, air.

The similarities between Giedion's and Rowe's writings may not be their most striking feature, but they are arresting enough for us to wonder why, on the evidence of these particular examples, the two historians should so often be presented as occupying opposing ideological positions. Both have a tendency to interpret modern architecture in terms of painting, and both, in their descriptions, rigorously bracket out everything other than visual/tactile impressions. This formal/visual emphasis is, thus, not restricted to Giedion's later writings from *Space, Time, and Architecture* onward, as some critics have claimed. Both historians are also particularly interested in the work of Le Corbusier—the one modernist who used painting as a testing ground for architectural ideas, and whose buildings—though they are completely architectural—explore forms which, in making use of the potential inherent in new materials, departed most radically from the tectonic tradition. Giedion and Rowe and Slutzky both struggle to give verbal expression to their strong visual feelings in the presence of Le Corbusier's architecture. Their "slots of space" and "cubes of air" are intended for the attentive viewer, not for "les yeux qui ne voient pas," nor for Benjamin's distracted user.

Notes

1   Richard Wagner, *My Life*, vol. 2 (London: Constable, 1911), 629.
2   Stephane Mallarmé, "Crise de vers," quoted in Philippe Junod, *Transparence et opacité: Essai sur les fondements théoriques de l'art moderne: pour une nouvelle lecture de Konrad Fiedler* (Lausanne: Éditions L'Age d'homme, 1975), 193.
3   This interpretation is close to that of Yve-Alain Bois in his discussion of Mondrian in *Painting as Model* (Cambridge, MA: MIT Press, 1990), "The De Stijl Idea," 102–106.
4   See Tim Benton, *Les Villas de Le Corbusier 1920–1930* (Paris: Philippe Sers, 1984), 165–189.

"In a funny way, we sabotaged the possibility of a third 'Transparency' essay through opposite directions. For at that time we had very strong differences of opinion—me as a modernist and Colin as a classicist. . . .

Colin's readings of Palladio and of history were fascinating, but the intention of the articles was to speculate about architecture's future, not its past!"

TO REASON WITH ONE'S VISION

Robert Slutzky
in conversation with Emmanuel Petit[1]

Your "Transparency" essays had a big impact on the way modern architecture has been conceptualized in American academia since the 1960s. Written in 1955–56 and first published in Yale's Perspecta *in 1963, these texts added new levels of sophistication to the reading of architectural form. Deriving their hypotheses from cubism and neoplasticism, your articles were among the first to introduce a critique of immaculate clarity presumed by modern architecture, and to speculate in favor of a double entendre. Metaphorically extended, your argument criticized the simplistic literal reification of the world, instead of which you proposed a method of layered "reading." Was this set of ideas only possible because of the interdisciplinary collaboration between Rowe, trained as an architect, and you, as a painter?*

Yes, that text could only have been written through the collaboration of an architect and a painter. I came into the relationship with Colin fresh from Yale, where I studied a fair amount of art history, including a seminar on educational theories. This led me to perceptual psychology, a subject which I think is very important for people dealing in visual matters to understand. Thus, the issue of transparency was already present in my work. My painting allowed me to see visual structures in both painting and architecture. Rowe wrote his article on Le Corbusier and Palladio five years prior to our meeting. That essay displayed Colin's ability to skip through large chunks of historical time to make comparisons of syntactic similarities hidden within disparate styles. Clearly, Colin, too, was sympathetic to the possibilities of the rich dialectic relationships between painting and architecture. When Colin and I were asked to go teach at the school of architecture at Austin, Texas, he taught advanced architectural studio, and occasionally history and theory. I was hired to teach first-year freehand drawing, two and three-dimensional design, and, later, color. Rowe, Bernhard Hoesli, and John Hejduk had major input in the upper-year studio courses, whereas Lee Hirsche and I, and later Rubin, completely reformed the first-year design pedagogy. The diversity of our group of educational imports was quite interesting. Hoesli had worked in Le Corbusier's office, and he came to

America seeking out Frank Lloyd Wright's architecture. Colin came to America to study with Hitchcock, and later took cross-country trips to British Columbia and the West Coast, before coming to Austin. I was a Miesian before I looked at Le Corbusier's architecture, and with Colin's help, I discovered certain insights into Corb's painting and architecture. Le Corbusier was an architect, but also a painter; in fact, he was the only architect who seriously painted—consciously of modernist aesthetics. In that sense, it was paradigmatic to have a painter and an architect coauthor the "Transparency" articles.

How did you develop your interest in architecture, and by extension, what brought you to Texas?

I had been interested in neoplastic self-referentiality from my experiences in painting at Yale. It dealt with intrinsically defined structural conditions that, in composition, emit dynamic plasticities. My notion of aesthetic time was measured by the engrossment of the viewing retina, which ideally would be frontal to the composition. That was my background. To answer your question very simply: One day in the summertime, having already received my MFA degree, I was walking down the hall at the Arts & Architecture building at Yale, and the dean thrust his head out of the hall window and said, "Slutzky, how would you like to teach in Texas?" And I jokingly said, "Where is that?" I had been through Texas, and I asked the dean, "Fine, where in Texas?" He said, "Austin, University of Texas, School of Architecture. Lee Hirsche is already down there, and he is waiting for you to say yes." So with a minimal delay in traveling to Texas, I very soon boarded an American Airlines plane, went down to Dallas, then changed to a DC3 run by Braniff to Austin, and I hooked up with architects to explore similar topics I had been introduced to in painting.

Once in Austin, the chemistry between the different characters was right; each person felt very positively about the other persons. I got along with John Hejduk, because he was from the Bronx and I was from Brooklyn, and he was six feet six inches tall, and I was five feet six inches tall; he was an architect who had pretensions to be a painter, and I was a painter who had pretensions to be an architect. People always say to me, "Why didn't you get into architecture?" I say, "Well, because I am trying to build on a two-dimensional plane."

Did you know Rowe before going to Austin? Were you aware of the essays he had written before the Texas years, such as "Mannerism and Modern Architecture"?

No, I may have seen Rowe in New Haven across the street. He looked familiar to me when I met him in Texas, but I couldn't remember where I had seen his face. And I was totally ignorant about his writings prior to meeting him. Thus, I read his essays with great enthusiasm shortly after we decided to share an apartment in Austin to get the "Transparency" articles written. When Colin and I decided to live together to do the papers in 1955, I also got a very nice studio at the back of the house so that I could do my painting, do my thinking, my writing, and my teaching. It was wonderful! I got to Austin more or less coincidentally, but when I went there, it was more than just a job! I discovered the cast of characters who were hired with me to rethink the pedagogy; I felt quite energetic and totally dedicated to the task of the reformulation that we intended to instate. I was particularly fascinated by my

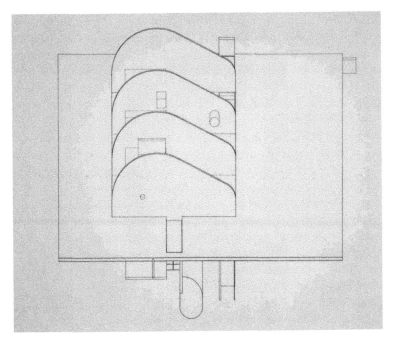

FIGURE 32   John Hejduk, Wall House 1: Worm's eye view (1968–77). Reprographic copy, 89 × 92.5 cm

Credit: Courtesy of John Hejduk fonds, Collection Centre Canadien d'Architecture / Canadian Centre for Architecture, Montréal, DR1998:0077:036

cohorts. It was a little bit like a movie, where five people would come accidentally into each other's lives. I met Colin in a very casual way. In the course of discussions around lunchtime in the faculty lunchroom, the subject of painting came up: the subject of space and painting, of the flatness of contemporary painting, of the quest for autonomy of the two-dimensional plane vis-à-vis Mondrian. Cubism came into discussion because it was heavy and made space through that heaviness. By comparison of soups, Renaissance space had the clarity of a consommé, an absolutely pure broth, whereas Cubist space was heavy pieces. Pieces of Minestrone were floating at the top and then would disappear in the heaviness of space.

When my contract expired and was not renewed (so it was too with Hejduk and Rowe), I went back up north and found employment at I.M. Pei's office, working in a graphic design section coincidentally run by, and peopled by, Yalies. The time during which our teaching in Texas took place, the middle of the 1950s, was very critical for all kinds of reasons that constituted the matrix of larger sociopolitical events. There was the end of the Korean war; there was a witch hunt, where left-wing radicals were being hunted by the government; there were South American and Central American intrigues; Castro came into power in 1959; the world was facing off between two supergiants; there was the imminence of nuclear war; there was an anxiety disturbing the tranquility of life. There was a confrontation of societies between Kennedy and Krushchev, and then the missile crisis in 1963. I am trying to say that it was an anxious moment. The conditions in Texas were almost isolated. It was removed from any larger city context. Austin was a slightly more sophisticated city than Dallas because it was the state capital. The University of Texas was a major institution so it was a good place to institute our program. The worldly problems just mentioned were somehow bracketed, enabling us to put our entire efforts into this pedagogical change without having to act on problems that were much more palpable in the big cities in America. In the big cities, the newspaper headline was always in front of you and the anxiety was always there. Austin was pacific, sedated, and we could concentrate more clearly. That was an important part of the Texas experiment. This was the frame that made our experiments possible.

While your experience as a painter was critical to introducing new modes of analysis and production in architecture, the methods and discourses of architecture must also have affected your view of painting; how did your time in Austin feed back into your painting?

More than feeding back into my painting, the correlation of two- and three-dimensional design was very important in my teaching in the first-year studio. What was a point or a line in two-dimensional design became column and wall in three dimensions. It was the handwriting, the signage that was different; architecture uses one further dimension. A painting uses an illusion to create space; this illusion is the result of the composition of the painting. Composition is the result of the dialectics of color and drawing. The plasticity and the composition ambiguously give you different readings at different moments. But the major distinction between painting and architecture is that painting has no bodily functions, whereas architecture serves at least one function. Painting is more perceptual, whereas architecture involves more physical mobility. You could not stand in front of a building and look at it like you are looking at a painting. You could, and you could derive pleasure from it, and in fact, in the second article we consider San Lorenzo in that way. It is an analysis of Michelangelo's facade, which really talks about treating the facade as if it were a painting.

When you talk about phenomenal transparency you are dependent on the existence of a frontal picture plane in order to be visually stimulated and to achieve structural ambiguity. Yet the mobile perception of architecture does not usually provide the frontality for the viewer inherent in painting; on the contrary, architecture provides a sequence of views. How do you understand this difference that makes the transparency argument pertinent to architecture?

Painting always requires a frontal engagement. Frontality, as described by Clement Greenberg, is a thickened and taut pictorial plane which is activated by color and drawing in nearly infinite numbers of configurations. It is true that architecture is intended for circulation and usage and is therefore much more complicated in the sense that it has to choreograph the vision of the spectator. However, architecture could be more structurally self-referential, in which case it would reestablish façades in a more compositional, dynamic way. Color and light could do so much to foreground this perception of the architecture, but architects have not really taken color or light into account; color in architecture is put in at the end of the equation. But

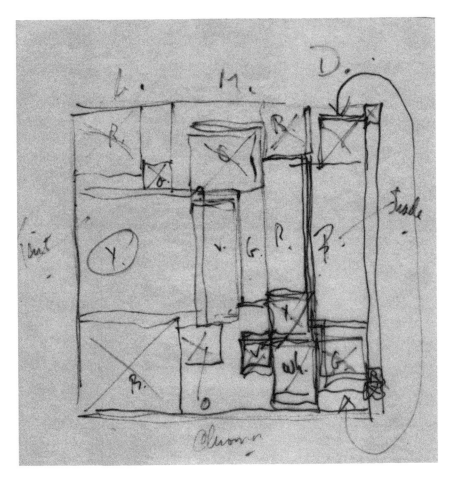

FIGURE 33   Robert Slutzky, Homage to Bach, sketch (1973)

Credit: Courtesy Joan Ockman

generally, the frontal view is the most important view in terms of establishing pos-sible façade-like configurations lying behind it. In other words, within the definition of façade are indicators of frames of information. It is not just pictorial as such, as if playing with shapes; it leads to an understanding of the structure of a building. The very function of a building and the function of space are organized in a number of ways in which phenomenal transparency comes into play. Architecture is a synthesis of all the different aspects of program, structure, and site. It addresses all of these issues either in secrecy or out in the open. Out in the open would imply glazing. But that is not necessarily what we are talking about. Glazing is what Gropius used in the Bauhaus building so that you could see through the wall. You could see that the floor slabs were cantilevered. We considered that a less meaningful way of revealing the structure of the building. It is a charming dematerialization of the object, but what

FIGURE 34 Robert Slutzky, Homage to Bach, painting (1973–74)
Credit: Courtesy Joan Ockman

we were looking for was a more poetic establishment of meaning in architecture that takes in other aspects besides purely painterly structures or compositions. I think the mistake of architects is to freeze an image and to let that image speak like a painting or a photograph might. That is to say that it is a mistake when there is a preferred point of view, and that point of view is then established and worked around.

Giedion's description of Gropius's Bauhaus building does not assume a static point of view!

In the "Transparency" essays we clarify what we thought to be a semantic error on the part of Giedion. Giedion's role is an interesting one, because if you look at the history, he was one of the first to come on this thing called modernism and make himself at home. Giedion's *Space, Time, and Architecture* was, at the time, the Bible of the modernist period. Colin looked at the very famous juxtaposition of Picasso's "L'Arlésienne" with the corner of Gropius's Bauhaus building, and we thought this is not true; this is syllogistic, this is not deep at all. There is a much different space and time; there is a fourth dimension in all that, and people ought to make a serious proposition about it. I just think that Colin and I agreed that comparing Picasso to Gropius, as Giedion suggested, was a terrible mistake. Furthermore, to use the name "cubism" to describe the Bauhaus building, which is essentially more of a constructivist thing, was wrong in our minds. The Bauhaus building is closer to Moscow than it is to Paris. And we didn't like the muddying of the definitions and the geography. Now, there are certain German artists that have crossed the boundary line, like

Kurt Schwitters. He, to me, is a cubist-Dada composer of wonderful compositions through collage. There are not many French who could be considered constructivists. The interesting jump across the Rhine aesthetically reflects the French and German confusion that I think Giedion was prey to.

How would you characterize your relationship to formalism as opposed to Rowe's?

Peter Eisenman is a formalist; Colin flirted with formalism. I don't think Colin was actually a formalist, if you mean formalism as I might apply it to painting. Colin abhorred the lack of representation. In the end, I think, he drifted back to representation completely. I am probably a formalist; I work on what I call color/structure in painting. In 1984, I had a show at Modernism gallery in San Francisco; it included fifteen paintings. For the catalogue of that exhibition I coauthored a piece called "Color/Structure/Painting" with Joan Ockman, which seeks to amplify the thinking of painting as a self-referential and therefore formalist activity. The idiosyncratic aspects of color are used as conceptual ammunition.

You had projected to write a third article on transparency, yet that one never made it beyond a rough sketch. Could you interpret this as symptomatic of your conceptual drift apart from Rowe?

I was easing out of the relationship with Rowe at the time he got to Cornell. The third article was never written, because by that time, Colin and I had different interests from each other. I remember Colin wanted to pull the third article back into classicism and I wanted to pull it into modernism, and there would be a fundamental split. Ideologically we drifted apart. I pursued my dreams, and he pursued his. When Colin embraced Léon Krier as an important architect, I realized that there was an irreconcilable cleavage separating Colin from me. In retrospect it all has to do with his latent suspicion of modernism; he thought modernism was too strict. He felt that modernism was a threat to history. Colin sensed that classical architecture allowed for infinite combinations, and he felt threatened by the notion of championing modernism. Therefore, he amplified his love for classical architecture. I could not agree with that. And I must confess that he never looked too hard at painting. He used painting more in the metaphorical sense, and he was not involved in the physical transaction with the canvas if it was non-representational. The stuff that he collected is an indicator of his taste; Colin had more of a premodern art collector's mind.

The first article is about the past, and about what was misnamed; the second one is about configurational ambiguities, but we also brought in classicism—San Lorenzo being an example of that. Colin's readings of Palladio and of history were fascinating, but the intention of the articles was to speculate about architecture's future, not its past! The speculations on San Lorenzo were the main addition from the first to the second article. For the third article, I would have gravitated toward Le Corbusier's La Tourette; it is a wonderful building to talk about metaphorical images and ambiguities. Rowe published an article called "Revisiting La Tourette," and he had the opportunity to talk about the things that I thought were important, but he didn't. He was interested in these pyrotechnical ways to describe a building.

When Corbusier died, incidentally, Colin and Robert Venturi went at each other. Colin was very critical of Venturi's mathematics building at Yale while Vincent Scully came into the act to defend Venturi. Colin was still using modernism as a way of critiquing Venturi's postmodernism. At that time, I was sympathetic to Colin's zeal, and I think it is a horrible building that Venturi designed, frankly. But after that there was just a slow drifting apart from Colin. I would see Colin occasionally, and every two or three years he would call. No longer was there a pedagogical or educational reason to associate with Colin, and frankly, as much as he has to offer in the history of architecture and the culture of architecture, we went in two different directions.

In a funny way, we sabotaged the possibility of a third "Transparency" essay through opposite directions. For at that time we had very strong differences of opinion—me as a modernist and Colin as a classicist. Whereas I looked into formalist possibilities in composition, Colin really was looking to substantiate a very developed consciousness of architectural history, which would give him the possibility to dig into the past and not postulate about the future necessarily. Therefore, the third essay was never written.

The intellectual difference also pertained to Rowe's growing interest in "collage," which would then lead to the "Roma Interrota" exhibition and to Collage City!

It was already before that. Colin would occasionally call me at 2:30 or 3:00 in the morning, and he would be totally inebriated. During one of those conversations I said the name of the book should not be *Collage City*, but *Montage City*. "Montage" has to do with representation, whereas "collage" has to do with the intrinsic structure of the material. Montage takes sociopolitical events and manipulates them in a way, whereas collage has to do with somewhat contiguous contours—forms which extract maximum meaning from each other. Collage seemed to me an inappropriate term. He liked "collage," but collage was really the invention of cubism, Picasso, and Braque.

When I worked for Pei, Colin also worked at I.M. Pei's office in the city-planning section, but did not stay for very long. Colin also went to Cooper to teach a couple of history courses. My contact with Colin eroded, because he drifted to his milieu, as I did to mine, and we got together again at Cornell. Hejduk would come to Cornell too. And people said, "Watch it, the Texas Rangers are coming again." But Colin went to England for a couple of years, and my contact with him was then minimal.

What guided your eventual interest in Le Corbusier, as opposed to Mies and Gropius?

I was very interested in Mies. Mies was using literal transparency, but he wasn't calling himself a cubist. Mies and Le Corbusier were two architects whom I took very seriously. The more I got involved in architectural thinking and critiquing, the more I liked Le Corbusier. Le Corbusier is unreachable by his contemporaries because he was a painter endowed with great creativity and he fused his painting into his architecture. Le Corbusier's Pavillon Suisse is wonderfully poetic; it is composed of different planes of vision. It starts with a curved rubble wall, then the wall becomes solid and unfenestrated, then the back wall is fenestrated—punched by squarish windows—and then there is glass. That is a wonderful take on the Renaissance! Le Corbusier turned it 90 degrees, and so the rubble wall, which would

FIGURE 35   Le Corbusier et Pierre Jeanneret, Pavillon Suisse, Cité internationale universitaire, Paris (1929–33)

Credit: © F.L.C. / ADAGP, Paris / Artists Rights Society (ARS), New York 2014

be the base of a Renaissance palazzo, is now the frontal plane or the entry plane. Entry is also signified on the front with the use of *pilotis*. The interesting thing is the metaphor of a *pas de deux*: the male part, which is rubble solid, is a cantilever system holding on to the slab. The biggest cantilever is to the park side, fully glazed. When you look at a section of the Pavillon Suisse, it is like a male dancer holding a female dancer in extension. The building metaphorically becomes bodies. So one can talk about a *pas de deux* in Corbusier's architecture. You cannot use that expression in Mies's architecture.

When Hoesli translated your and Rowe's essay into German, he wrote a commentary about it in a book he published at the Institute for the History and Theory of Architecture at the Swiss Federal Institute of Technology in Zurich. What is your take on his appropriation of your "transparency" concept? Hoesli translated the analytical tool of phenomenal transparency into a synthetic and operative instrument for architectural design, and concluded his comment with examples of student design exercises. This "form" was not to be the result but the catalyst of the design. Was this kind of "operative theory" inscribed already in the Rowe and Slutzky version of transparency, or did Hoesli's instrumentalist view stretch your interest in transparency too far?

It was definitely stretched too far! I mean, using Frank Lloyd Wright to talk about cubist space is ridiculous. I think one of the errors architects make—including some of my best friends like Hoesli or Hejduk—is to analyze a Juan Gris painting, for example, and build from that. It is like taking a pin, catching a butterfly, pinning the butterfly to the wall, and staring at the butterfly even though the butterfly is dead. You cannot do that to painting! You cannot freeze painting. So Hoesli freezes a still life by Le Corbusier by slicing it up. But you can't cut up a phenomenally transparent painting. The same is true of phenomenally transparent architecture. Once you see three sides of the Pavillon Suisse, the structure of the fourth side becomes self-evident. You don't need to see that fourth facade; you *know* it is there and what it looks like because you can sense the way the planes are gradated and distributed in space.

Some time ago, you told me about a photo of the faculty at Austin. In the photo, everyone was looking at the camera except Rowe, who was looking up at the ceiling. Tell me how you interpreted the image. What does it tell us about Rowe's character, or about his presence in Austin?

The photo suggested to me that he was, in a funny way, stuck with the commoners there, so to speak. He was put into the assemblage of ordinariness. I read it as a little boyish gesture of not wanting to be pinned down, of wanting to be ethereal, looking at the clouds. What comes together in that picture in my mind is something mysterious about Colin. He had the ability to apprehend and convey original ideas. He was quite erudite, as you know. He knew an enormous amount of European culture and history. And he had a mind that was like a library. He could cite the page that an illustration was on and whether it was on the left side or the right side in the book. He was uncanny in that respect.

In 1956 Rowe, Hejduk, and you left Texas, and you said you were fired from the school . . .

Yes, it had to do with the program. The old guard could not wait to see us leave. We were Young Turks and they were old farts, and some were quite hostile. When I taught drawing, I had a full-time co-professor as my assistant who resented me like you cannot believe. So that made teaching psychologically difficult. Harwell Harris made a very big mistake in making his old-guard assistants to his young rebels. You can imagine the old faculty saying, "Let's get rid of those seditious guys." The miraculous thing was that in two years we established all of that pedagogy that was ready for further qualification. We all devoted our entire energy to build a new program, and we all pitched in.

Hejduk and you were again together at the Cooper Union in New York from 1968 to 1990. At one moment, you expressed your discontent with the ways in which "creativity" was promoted there . . . which you thought was more appropriate for the salon than for a school of architecture. You spent two decades at the Cooper Union, but from 1981 on, you did not teach architecture, but switched to the art department instead. You seem to have had an interest in structure, whereas Hejduk developed his interest in poetics; only you were not convinced that poetry could inform, but only result from architectural structure. Tell us about the conceptual divergence between you and Hejduk?

My expectation was that the transplantation of the ideas from Texas to Cooper Union would lead to a less salon-like atmosphere. I thought there would be more possibilities in the actual realization of architecture and architectural program. The school at Cooper Union was built on the premise that the Texas experiment could be elaborated in a realistic way to train architects, that what we did in Texas could be refined and become the new pedagogy in architecture. I thought Cooper Union needed more pragmatic vertebrae. To me, schools are not about promoting styles. John and I argued with each other over this. I think there is a poetics of structure and function in architecture; one can even explore the poetics of a bathroom. So you are right, I would sometimes be the tougher critic on juries, asking, "Why is the bathroom so far from the bedroom?" Or, "Why isn't there a washroom close to the entry?" You know, the kind of everyday things that architects deal with. For a while, I functioned as a harsh architectural critic. Being a faculty member in an architecture school but not being an architect, I enjoyed the liberty of saying these things to architects, though never in a malicious way.

Was there a specific moment in time when you thought the concepts you elaborated in "Transparency" lost its critical power—that something would have to be changed or added to the theory so that the strong visual orientation of the argument could reenergize architecture once again?

No, there is no precise moment. For me there was a slow drift away after coauthoring the two articles, based primarily on the educational experiences that Colin had in his life and I in mine, which is to say that I used phenomenal transparency to teach painting and fine arts. I don't think the argument is dead. It will be studied for the way in which one reasons with one's vision. The articles exemplify a critical attitude concerning the plastic arts, and such an analysis can produce exciting results. In other words, it is a certain methodology of criticism that still has validity, even though you might disagree with the conclusions. In a way, it is repeatedly reaffirming the constancy of vision and the primacy of perception—which is related to the thoughts of Maurice Merleau-Ponty. I think Merleau-Ponty's title *Primacy of Perception* is absolutely correct. Language has to follow the percept, not the other way round. It is important to sense the reality, or the actuality, of the stuff out there, which then can be somewhat addressed through language. The ineffability of art should remain supreme. You talk about a painting, and the painting says, "Don't talk; look at me." You may think sentences, you may think paragraphs, and you may even think books, but the painting outlasts them. In architecture you have the same condition. There is an enormous amount of critical theory in architecture, but I distrust words to a large degree when it comes to painting and architecture. The point is that architecture is a tactile-perceptual reality. You cannot see all the nuances right away. The architectural object is occluded in a way that prevents you from understanding the profundity of the construct. In that sense, whether or not you agree with some of the conclusions that Colin and I came up with is incidental. The issue is the way the world out there is perceived, how it is appreciated sensuously.

So did you think that Rowe, who was foremost a theorist and a historian, was entangled in words and concepts and that he did not take the primacy of the percept seriously enough?

Colin was trained as an architect, and he designed a few things. But I think that he was really looking for pedigree, he was looking to see whether or not a building could somehow be seen as birthed by history. And as you know that is not the thesis of a constructivist, or a suprematist, or a De Stijl–ist, all of whom believed in severing modern art from history. I am out here painting my paintings, and no one is telling me to stop, and I am painting my paintings not as a polemic, but as a resurrection of the musicality that is residual in painting. Painting can achieve what music has achieved over the centuries, which is the wonderful manufacture of aesthetic, temporal conditions born from hermetic adjustments. There is time in art just as there is in music. My perception of Rowe is that he became enamored of classical principles in architecture and in painting. I don't think he would analyze a painting the way I would. He would see it more as a stylistic phenomenon, epitomizing a certain cultural order. For example, Rowe introduced me to mannerism in architecture. I then looked back into mannerism in painting. But in trying to understand mannerism in painting, my aim wasn't to use, say, Bronzino to establish a pedigree for Fernand Léger, Jackson Pollock, or any other twentieth-century painter. I don't think like that. I'm more interested in understanding syntactic similarities between mannerist and modern paintings, if there are any. But at the same time, we know that painting is beyond syntax.

The analytical eye tends to read the text in a way that closes down perception unnecessarily. This unfortunately produces a lot of talk about architecture, and very little understanding of the deep structures of architecture. Of course, architecture is out in the public in a political and social domain, while painting is there by itself

FIGURE 36 "Rowe's Ghost"; Amtrak train ticket stubs with uncanny name confusion: "Rowe" instead of "Slutzky" (2001)

Credit: Courtesy Joan Ockman

in a room with no windows; it's open to the perception of one artist. It has just as much validity of existence as architecture but it realizes its concepts in a different way than architecture.

With regard to Rowe's uncanniness, there is one anecdote I need to tell you, and I am not manufacturing this. A year and a half after Colin died, I was talking about him to my daughter late at night. The next morning, I went with Joan to 30th Street Station in Philadelphia to purchase a ticket to New York. I paid with my credit card, and my ticket was handed to me. And on the ticket, which had my correct card number, was not my name but Rowe's!! Now, mathematically speaking, what chance in a trillion is there that this kind of confusion could happen? But it did happen and I still have the ticket stubs to prove it! I suddenly had a very strange feeling of being haunted by Colin . . .

Note

1   This text is the outcome of a series of conversations recorded in Elkins Park, Pennsylvania, in 2002. It was edited to its current form by Joan Ockman in 2012.

"Architecture is a form of sociology, we were told and, if concerned with buildings at all, a kind of social engineering at best. . . .

The idea of form as neither an end in itself nor as a result of design but as an instrument of design seems still quite difficult to grasp."

TRANSPARENT FORM-ORGANIZATION AS AN INSTRUMENT OF DESIGN[1]

Bernhard Hoesli

In my commentary of 1968 I was first of all concerned with generalizing the concept of phenomenal transparency which Rowe and Slutzky had established by evolving it from intense contemplation and a tightly reasoned morphological analysis of two Le Corbusier buildings: the villa Les Terrasses at Garches and the League of Nations competition project.

Above all it was my intention to show that the generalization "transparency exists where a locus in space can be referred to two or several systems of relations—where the assignment remains undetermined and the belonging to one or the other remains a matter of choice" is a universally applicable criterion for characterizing form organization just as for instance symmetry or asymmetry. To ask if there is transparency in a form-organization is like applying a piece of litmus paper and permits the distinction and exact description of a quality which might go unnoticed or, if not, can only be circumscribed in an elaborate and cumbersome way.

To apply the test of transparency is part of a morphological approach that holds the exact description of a phenomenon as the necessary and indispensable prerequisite for any insight, understanding or knowledge. It belongs to the great tradition of systematizing effort that, say, in the case of botany, culminated in the sovereign work of Linné.

The attempt to describe buildings or urban patterns independently from their historical context, to see them side by side across periods of stylistic differences and to insist on a common quality in works from widely differing epochs, produced by distinct social, technical and political conditions may disturb or shock and dismay the historian. But of course it is not proposed to remove a particular building from its historical and cultural context; to look for transparency is merely a possibility to disengage part of its characteristic form.

The concept of transparency invites to see differences that can provide the key to understand qualities of uniqueness or similarity. And, especially at a time when architects seem intent to consider history as a self-service store stocked with an

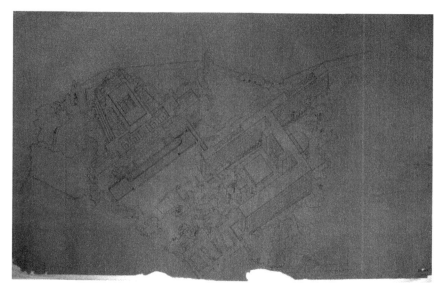

FIGURE 37   Le Corbusier, League of Nations, Geneva (1927)

Credit: © F.L.C. / ADAGP, Paris / Artists Rights Society (ARS), New York 2014

inexhaustible supply of motifs and forms, it should be useful and might be sobering to welcome precise tools that help to reduce motif, form and effect to their "essential significant facts and forces,"[2] so that we can, starting from these, create the motifs and authentic forms out of the constituent factors of our own time conceptually, leaving out of count flirtation or abuse on a perceptional level.[3]

With the numerous examples where phenomenal transparency once singled out can be observed, I then, in 1968, endeavored to convey the idea that transparency, defined as a state of relationships between the elements of a form organization, can also be considered and used as a means of organizing form. That aspect should have been stressed, the idea made explicit. Soon after the publication of my commentary schools of architecture entered the rapids of "la contestation." Architecture is a form of sociology, we were told and, if concerned with buildings at all, a kind of social engineering at best. There could not possibly be an interest in architectural form, which was declared of no importance at all or "unmasked" as a device of oppression to the advantage of the interest of a ruling class and to the detriment of the common good. Interest in problems of architectural form was held in contempt. Space was denounced as architect's fiction.

Nobody can complain about a lack of interest in form today. It has come back with a vengeance. To the impairment and impoverishment of all the rest "Functionalism" is criticized because it is imputed that it considered form as result; now form is considered an agent of typology or a precedent at one's disposal. Architectural form must claim "autonomy"—we are now told—that however it doesn't really seem to enjoy.

The idea of form as neither an end in itself nor as a result of design but as an instrument of design seems still quite difficult to grasp.

The Predicament of Form

One evidently creates forms in order to designate and inform. Something that is, is designated for someone whom one wishes to inform about something that is. And he who tells wants to be understood. So there are two possibilities to corrupt architectural form: The corruption of its relation to the reality of the use of the building, to what it is—or the corruption of its nature as information.

Obviously there are several possibilities to explain the origin of form in architecture, to define the relation of form and use or to specify the connection between form and "function." They all purport to relate the inward functioning and purpose of a building to its external expression.

Now if architectural form is "autonomous," if it should be divorced from the intent and content of a building, emancipated from a palpable relation to its use—there is a loss of truth, hence morality.

Two opposing views of the relation of content and form claim our attention today, and both claim orthodoxy—one in the defensive and engaged in rear guard actions, the other in full vigor and expanding in various disguises.

There is first the supposedly "functionalist" position contending that "Instead of forcing the functions of every sort of building into a general form, adopting an outward shape for the sake of the eye or of association, without reference to the inner distribution, let us begin from the heart as the nucleus, and work outward. The most convenient size and arrangement of the rooms that are to constitute the building being fixed, the access of the light that may, of the air that must be wanted, being provided for, we have the skeleton of our building."[4] Or, as Louis Sullivan put it in the *Autobiography of an Idea*: ". . . the function of a building must predetermine and

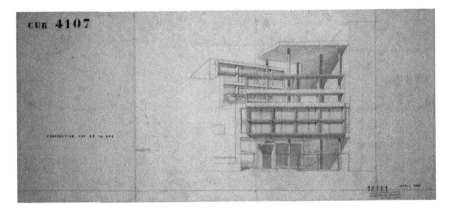

FIGURE 38 Le Corbusier, Villa Curutchet, perspective drawing of front facade, La Plata, Argentina (1949–53); Hoesli worked on this project while employed in Le Corbusier's office.

Credit: © F.L.C. / ADAGP, Paris / Artists Rights Society (ARS), New York 2014

organize its form." That was based on observation of biological growth and form in nature and certainly must have been meant as analogy. It prefigured Le Corbusier's poetic metaphor "Un édifice est comme une bulle de savon. Cette bulle est parfaite et harmonieuse si le souffle est bien réparti, bien réglé de l'intérieur. L'extérieur est le résultat de l'intérieur."[5] That understanding of the relation of purpose and form in architecture established the connection of cause and effect. The form-reality of a building is seen as a function of its envisaged use in the sense of the mathematical term function: $y = f(x)$, a variable depending on constants and variables, the old "form follows function."

The second, so-called "rational," understanding maintains in exact opposition to the first that "function follows form." And there is a coherent argument based on observation to demonstrate the validity and usefulness of this view. Most buildings in a historical context demonstrate the basic continuity of form to which ever-changing use was adapted; the Diocletian Palace of Spalato, the stadion of Domitian of Imperial Rome, the list of glorious fragments of fabric and of artifacts that bear witness is almost endless.

When the first explanation proclaims in the most radical formulation of Mies van der Rohe "*we refuse to recognize problems of form*, but only problems of building. Form is not the aim of our work, but only the result. Form, by itself, does not exist . . ."[6]—the second declares that in architecture *there are only problems of form* and design means to transform, to adapt form through deformation and by quoting typological form-precedent, while the usefulness of a building will take care of itself as a matter of course.

Of course this seemingly revolutionary stance in the "postmodern" late sixties was shrewdly anticipated in the early fifties in the relaxed, more sophisticated, less polemical and possibly slightly puzzled observation of Matthew Nowicki that "form follows form."

Both positions in opposition mentioned in this argument have however this in common: they both are "either–or" and are concerned with establishing what has ascendancy, takes precedence or must claim priority—purpose or form. Frank Lloyd Wright's contribution to the collection: "*form and function are one*" indicates a possible position outside the polemic. If rendered operative this formula can lead to the hunch that suggests the idea that form is an instrument of design. *Form* in architecture could be *understood as instrument*—neither as typologically preexisting original position to which all else has to become subordinate, nor as following from premises as result.

Use and form of a building or urban context must be understood as but two different aspects of the same thing, and to design means that they have to become fused through stubborn, patient work in a process of mutual adjustment, adaptation and reconciliation in which each is judiciously interpreted in terms of the other. This obviously presupposes a particular attitude of mind. One has to be willing to renounce a fixed point of view; one has to be prepared to see contrasting or even contradictory notions as not necessarily excluding each other and accept that "certainty" can only reside in a temporary stage in a sustained debate in which each partner supplements and completes the other's position in a dialogue of give and take, of this-as-well-as-that.

Excursus on the Concept of Architectural Space

Everything that is implied by the term "use," that is all activities for which a building is intended, is a manifestation in space as is everything that is implied by "form" of a building. Space can be said to be the common matrix of use and form. So it seems necessary at this point to introduce a concept of space to provide a possible reference for the further train of thought.

Concepts of space are inventions. They have their usefulness, life span and history. We can start with the axiomatic ascertainment that "space" is first of all an elementary existential experience of conscious man. "Taking possession of space is the first gesture of living things, . . . The occupation of space is the first proof of existence."[7] We can acknowledge that this is the space of Plato: "the mother and receptacle of all created and visible . . . things . . . , the universal nature which receives all bodies . . . and never in any way or any time assumes a form. . . ."[8] It hardly neither helps nor matters to call this "natural" space. Descartes made this "universal" space accessible in terms of arithmetics and geometry; in the second half of the 17th century, Newton succeeded in formulating the universal laws that govern in terms of physics the possible mechanics in this space. We can term this mathematical-physical space. It is homogeneous, isotropic and infinite. It seems that psychology too accepts this kind of space as the basic condition of perceptions. No need to point out that it possesses no animism, is not animate, that it can be neither "exploded" nor "compressed" and certainly does not "flow." It's just there. Nothing mysterious about it. It is.

To create architectural space man has to interfere in mathematical-physical space in order to claim, stake out or mark a particular part of it. Thus architectural space is made noticeable, it can be experienced, it is defined. One can distinguish two different kinds of space-definition.

First: space-defining elements (e.g. walls, screens, piers, columns) set bonds to, delimit, enclose, encircle, fence in, contain, a particular piece of mathematical-physical space that can be felt henceforth. A space-boundary or space-delimitation must be created and the sensation of space-definition is determined by the measure of enclosures a space-boundary provides. One can then distinguish interior, exterior, "inside" and "outside" space and space between objects.

Second: a space-defining element activates by its volumetric presence a locus in mathematical-physical space, it occupies space and thus by "dislodging space" makes that we experience space. Its corporeality suggests that we experience our bodily existence and thus experience space.

Part of the substratum of mathematical-physical space is transformed by being architecturally defined: it has become architectural space with distinguishing qualities and attributes.

It follows that space in terms of architecture is conceptually a continuous medium comprising the perceptually distinguished solid of mass and void of space.

As soon as we see and understand solid and void as equally participating in or equally constituent of a figure-ground continuity it is no longer necessary to insist on their perceptually antithetical nature. We know that buildings, volumes, contain space; in architecture "solids" are only colloquially solid mass. Space inside and between architectural objects is part of the same medium, the same whole. One might suggest by hint of analogy that "volume" or solid and "space" or void are but phenotypical aspects of genotypically continuous space.

This dualistic concept of a figure-ground continuity of solid and void as complementary aspects of space is, as all evidence reveals, the concept of *continuous space of Modern Architecture*. Frank Lloyd Wright arrived at it empirically from about 1893 to 1906, de Stijl presupposes it for its spatial inventions, Mies van der Rohe no less than Le Corbusier conceives and works in it[9]: continuous space is the common denominator in relation to which much of the obvious differences of their work can be assessed. It is the reference that permits distinction of species.

In view of this concept of continuous space the Nolli technique of showing the space of a square extending into the nave of a church or into the colonnade of a palazzo, though no less remarkable, seems only "natural" and obvious.

Unnecessary the invention of such innocently endearing and cleverly amusing notions such as "space and anti-space" or "positive space" (for void) and "negative space" (for mass)[10]—one a quite flirtatious and unnecessary reverence for nuclear physics, the other an only colloquially useful and not very helpful transfer of the device of positive and negative signs from arithmetic to the subject of space. There is of course no questioning the matter that is brought into focus by such attempts to distinguish nor doubting the necessity of distinction, but to term it thus seems weak, because in doing so one uses quite inadvertently a perceptual everyday colloquial distinction of mass and space to presumably attain conceptual vigor. I think it worthwhile to work with a general concept that admits of no exceptions but then provides for special conditions and explains them as special cases as such—rather than providing every single phenomenon with a new term that suggest a new notion. And, anyway, it may be useful to remember Bernard Berenson's impatient and slightly sarcastic passage in *Aesthetics and History*: ". . . So the art writing of the German-minded has been more and more dedicated to discussing space determination, space filling, space distortion, space this, space that. . . ."[11]

It may be that attention to space is the expression of an open society where plurality is accepted and recognized, where contradiction is not only tolerated but held in esteem as inherent in the *condition humaine* and where dialog is an indispensable technique for mutual advancement. And then, perhaps concentration on isolated objects is indulged in by a society seeking to escape complexity with the help of simplification of issues and in trying to find refuge in willingly accepted authority or in the surrender to "history." If these conjectures should not be refuted, if these assumptions are true—and, given the interest of the Neo-Rationalists in volume, their neglect of space and their unabated concern for the solitary object even in the context of an urban situation—we may cherish the hope that a persistent avoidance of all memory of "The Moment of Cubism"[12] and a continued evasion of the barely explored and yet inexhausted possibilities of Modern space will prevail for some time to come; or we can worry and regret that the "New World of Space"[13] has perhaps vanished for good.

The concept of a figure-ground relation of solid and void in *Continuous Space* permits conceptually effortless oscillation between the two opposing aspects of space, solid and void, which are not seen as mutually exclusive but mutually presupposing each other and being of equal value and enjoying "equal rights" as aspects or parts of the same whole. So buildings and spaces between buildings are seen as partners in a sustained debate, protagonists in a dialogue "who progressively contradict and clarify each other's meaning."[14] To move at ease in the space that this dualistic concept of space describes most certainly helps the designer who has to deal with plurality, complexity, contradiction—with the manifold demands of everyday reality.

For the present argument it would appear that a concept of space, that conceives of the world of space as consisting of the two but complementary aspects of solid and void, is the very matrix on which transparency can thrive. It is not suggested that the concept of Continuous Space is the prerequisite or one of the necessary conditions for the existence of transparency or for creating a transparent form organization. But to work with this concept just possibly reveals an inclusive mentality refusing an "either–or" approach, a willingness and capacity for conceiving and dealing with the "as-well-as"—just as a taste for transparent form organization might. The concept of continuous space and transparent form-organization can thus both be seen as manifestations of a frame of mind. One gives meaning to the other.

Transparency—Instrument of Design

Transparent form-organization should be considered as an instrument of design, as a technique for creating intelligible order as are for instance the use of axial addition, repetition or symmetry. Transparency as organization of form produces clarity as well as it allows for ambiguity and ambivalence. It assigns each part not only one definite position and distinct role in a whole but endows it with a potential for several assignments, each of which though distinct can be determined from time to time by deciding in which connection one chooses to see it. Transparency then is imposed order and freedom of choice at the same time. The transparent organization of ambiguousness would seem a particularly useful way to create order at a time seeking emancipation from obligation, at a time of multiple and often irreconcilable conditions for a building, and perhaps contradictory expectations that ought to be met by successful design. Transparency as form-organization is inclusive: it can absorb contradiction and local singularities, such as local symmetry for instance, without endangering the cohesion and readability of the whole.

A transparent organization of space has, because it allows and even encourages multiple readings of the interconnections between the parts of a whole system of related spaces, a built-in flexibility of use. Flexibility is provided and exists through possible interpretation, through flexible use of a supply of possibilities inherent in a given arrangement of spaces and not through physical flexibility of, say, movable partitions. Again we have the life-enhancing vigor of the tension between fact and implication, between physical fact and interpretation.

Since a transparent organization invites and encourages the fluctuation of multiple readings, and suggests individual interpretation, it activates and involves. The spectator remains not observer "on the outside," he becomes part of the composition through his participation. He enters a dialogue. He has to decide and in "reading" a facade, choosing one of several possible readings of the composition he is, at the same time, in his imagination, engaged in its creation.

If thus supremacy of the visual and its individual interpretation over the subject matter is assured, then meaning could be a quality that comes into being through accruing, through sedimentation, and not be "attached" to certain forms or motifs to which meaning is thought to be attributable by association or is believed to derive from precedent. Meaning can thus consist in the ad hoc or repeated identification of the beholder with the object. Meaning then blossoms from personal involvement, it

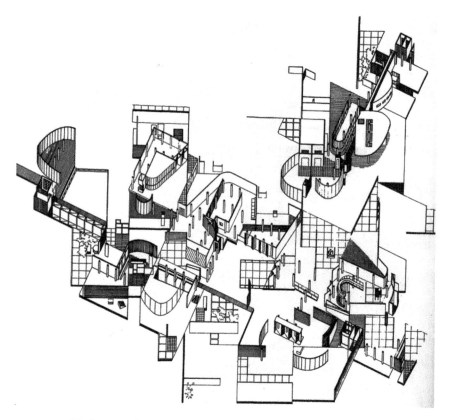

FIGURE 39 Mark Jarzombek, diploma thesis at the ETH in Zurich under Bernhard Hoesli, axonometric plan (1979–80)

Credit: © Mark Jarzombek

FIGURE 40 Mark Jarzombek, diploma thesis at the ETH in Zurich under Bernhard Hoesli, model (1979–80)

Credit: © Mark Jarzombek

is created in the act of focusing on one of the possible readings of form relations that are latent, inherent or implied in the form-organization.

It is for these reasons that at a time of presumably pluralistic expectations, of contradictory wants, of individual needs and demands and the mannerist penchant for inversion and allusion, transparent form-organization might be of particular value and should enjoy considerable favor where the desire to create inclusive form under contradictory conditions persists.

It would seem that transparent form-organization would be the instrument of design par excellence that permits collage as an attitude conducive to artifacts resulting from a technique that would render feasible "a way of giving integrity to a jumble of pluralistic references."[15] It would materialize collage as a state of mind encouraging the "politics of bricolage," activity that "implies a willingness to deal with the odds and ends left over from human endeavor."[16] Phenomenal transparency is a means of form-organization that permits to incorporate the heterogeneous elements in a complex architectural or urban tissue, to treat them as essential part of collective memory and not as embarrassment.

A Note on *Poché*

Poché, literally: blackened; parts of plan or section filled with black to indicate the parts of a structure that are cut, as could be done by stippling. We may get closer to the usefulness of that resurrected term if we think of *"l'oeuf poché"*–the poached egg. For if we connect the verb *"pocher"* with *"la poche,"* the pocket, then *"pocher"* can become *"mettre en poche"* and the past participle *"poché"* could be said to signify pocketed or "bagged," put into a bag, German: *eingesackt.* So, then "poché" would be an ideal shape put into a bag, surrounded with tissue. And that precisely seems to have happened with square, semicircle and other ideal shapes at the bottom of the Vatican Gardens.

And if we consider the imprint of structure on the plan as ground that acts to disengage the figures of the enclosed spaces—very similar to the "black lines" in a Mondrian that are perhaps all that's left from a black field after white and color rectangles have been placed on it—one may say that the procedure here presupposes apparently a primary interest in the object-figure and that one is intent on preserving its ideal form. One can then experience each individual space one at the time and one after the other. Poché is like the mortar joints between the individual stones and blocks of a rubble-wall. Attention is reserved for the part and there is, perhaps, less a comprehensive feel for the whole.

The whole very often remains but the sum of its parts or at least attention to the individual part enjoys supremacy over attention to the whole which is rather object than field. On one hand, a consciousness of parts, on the other an intuition of the whole. Poché as "joint" or transition taken as figure, obviously refers as an "inbetween" to the adjoining spaces that act against it—just as a locus in space in a transparent position that "can be referred to two or several systems." Aside from possible differences in scale one is acting in terms of mass, the other in terms of space; we recognize the joint as mass or as space, as solid or as void.

It would then appear that transparency and poché are related by inversion: in a transparent form organization there are spaces that refer to two or several systems just as poché does as "solid" mass in a complex whole consisting of several discrete spaces. In terms of the whole, their roles are equivalent, just as solid and void are in terms of continuous space. Poché is present as material, transparency as space—both are, though inverted and opposing as existence, equal as performance.

Notes

1 Bernhard Hoesli, "Addendum" (1982); from *Transparency*, Colin Rowe and Robert Slutzky; with a commentary by Bernhard Hoesli and an introduction by Werner Oechslin (Boston: Birkhäuser Verlag, 1997), 84–99. Reprinted with permission of Walter de Gruyter GmbH, Berlin.

2 Bernard Berenson, Italian Painters of the Renaissance, in *Meridian* 40, 1957, 180.

3 I use the term "authentic" as introduced by Christian Norberg Schultz. See "Towards an Authentic Architeture" in *The Presence of the Past*, London: Academy Editions, 1980, 21.

4 Horatio Greenough, *Form and Function*, Oakland, CA: University of California Press, 1947, 60, 61, xvii.

5 Le Corbusier, *Vers une Architecture*, Paris: Vincent Freal, reprint 1958, 146.

6 Philip Johnson, *Mies van der Rohe*, New York: The Museum of Modern Art, 1947, 184.

7 Le Corbusier, *New World of Space*, New York: Reynald and Hitchcock, 1948, 71.

8 Rudolf Arnheim, *The Dynamics of Architectural Form*, Oakland, CA: University of California Press, 1977, 9.

9 Arthur Drexler says of the Barcelona Pavilion: "Interior space becomes a fluid medium channeled between planes. Interior and exterior space, no longer rigidly opposed, are now simply degrees or modulations of the same thing." Arthur Drexler, *Mies van der Rohe* (Ravensburg, 1960) p. 15. See also Le Corbusier notes of the Pompeiian House in a remarkable sentence: "Il n'y a pas d'autres elements architecturaux de l'interieur: la lumiere et les murs qui la reflechissent en grande nappe et le sol qui est un mur horizontal. Faire des murs eclaires, c'est constituer les elements architecturaux de l'interieur." Le Corbusier, *Vers une Architecture*, Paris: Vincent Freal, reprint 1958, 150.

10 Steven Peterson, "Space and Anti-Space" in *The Harvard Review*, Vol I, MIT-Press, spring 1980, 89.

11 Bernard Berenson, *Aesthetics and History*, Doubleday Anchor, 1954, 97.

12 John Berger, *The Moment of Cubism*, London: Weidenfeld and Nicolson, 1969.

13 Le Corbusier, *New World of Space*, New York: Reynald and Hitchcock, 1948.

14 Colin Rowe's felicitous turn of phrase. Cf. *The Mathematics of the Ideal Villa and Other Essays*, Cambridge, MA: MIT Press, 1976, 194.

15 Colin Rowe and Fred Koetter, "Collage City," in *Architectural Review*, August 1975, 89.

16 Ibid., 83.

"It is my contention that if Rowe and Koetter so carefully avoided any mention of the cinema—the archetypal art form of the twentieth century—and resorted instead to a painterly analogy, it is because their argument is based on a deeply embedded belief that architecture and the city are the embodiment of permanence and stasis. Cinema is, by definition, about change and motion."

MONTAGE

Deconstructing Collage

Bernard Tschumi

Shot 1: *Two or Three Things I Know about Her*

In *Deux ou trois choses que je sais d'elle* (*Two or Three Things I Know about Her*, 1967), Jean-Luc Godard took a critical look at the transformation of the city and of modern life in the 1950s and 1960s.[1] Much as, in the mid-nineteenth century, Baron Georges-Eugène Haussmann had carved wide boulevards out of the narrow, convoluted streets of medieval Paris in response to the rise of industrialism and the resulting explosion of the urban population, Godard now asked if the housing crisis and the importation of an immigrant work force in the 1950s and 1960s similarly required a new form of urbanism. Decades earlier, Le Corbusier and Ludwig Hilberseimer, among others, had provided the possibility of a new model. The twentieth-century equivalent of the Haussmann plan was the *Plan Voisin* by Le Corbusier, with versions destined for implementation on the outskirts of Paris.[2]

Two or Three Things suggests that a new lifestyle ensues from urban transformation, marked by social estrangement and the unabashed consumerism celebrated in road signs and advertising. The film tells the story of a city in the making and of a young woman, Juliette, who prostitutes herself in order to participate in a lifestyle involving fashionable clothes, desirable commodities, and newly necessary domestic comforts, as defined by consumer culture.

The "Her," or *Elle*, is the Paris Region. The last shot of the film shows a model of the new city made out of Brillo detergent boxes and everyday consumer products, all of them together looking exactly like a Modern Movement plan of the period. "*Des tours et des barres*" was the contemporaneous motto of architects from Le Corbusier to Mies van der Rohe.

Shot 2: *Collage City*

In *Collage City*, written with Fred Koetter and published in 1978, Colin Rowe[3] opposed modernist urban planning and urban form to earlier historical models, which he considered to be more successful architecturally. His attack on modern urbanism represents an attack on its ideology as much as its form: "The city of modern architecture, both as psychological construct and as physical model, has been rendered tragically ridiculous." Rowe continues:

> By one interpretation, modern architecture is a hard-headed and hard-nosed undertaking. There is a problem, a specific problem, and there is an obligation, an obligation to science, to solve it in all its particularity; and so, while without bias and embarrassment we proceed to scrutinize the facts, then, as we accept them, we simultaneously allow these empirical facts to dictate the solution.[4]

He proceeds with another line of interpretation: there is also "the proposition that modern architecture is the instrument of philanthropy, liberalism, the 'larger hope' and 'the great good,'" often impelled by the idealism of "the counter-culture—life, people, community, and all the rest." Rowe concludes by presenting a dilemma of negative interpretation: "which of these two prospective programs for the future—the despotism of 'science' or the tyranny of the 'majority'—is the more completely repulsive is difficult to say."

Shot 3: Objective–Subjective Modernity

For *Two or Three Things*, Godard prepared a "commercial script," which summarized in a dozen pages twenty-four hours in the life of Juliette, a married woman with two young children living in a Modernist *grand ensemble* at La Courneuve, outside of Paris. In Godard's recounting, she drops her children off in the morning before heading out to work the city as a prostitute, a job that supports her multiplying consumerist desires. She returns every evening to her box of a home in the apartment block, surrounded on all sides by the cranes of construction sites. Godard also prepared a "non-commercial script" (one that, as he wrote, should "not [be] show[n] to potential financial partners"[5]), in which he explains the four elements of his cinema: (1) an objective description of objects and subjects, that is, buildings and people; (2) a subjective description of objects and subjects, through feelings; (3) a reason for structure ("1 + 2 = 3"), and (4) life, that is, bringing all components together as 1 + 2 + 3 = 4 ("When one lifts the skirt of the city, one sees its sex").

These "objective shots" include covers of books, billboards, housing slabs or towers, construction sites, gas stations, laundry soaps, and a long, hypnotic shot of the bubbling surface of hot coffee in a cup. The "subjective shots" are made up of scenes of Juliette's everyday life. Godard also experiments with dissociations between what the viewer sees on the screen and the descriptive voice-over of the soundtrack. "So Juliette goes and meets Robert who is completing his day at the gas station in the car park of the Champs Elysées, where he is a supervisor," says Godard, who intentionally links together two themes at a different scale—a moment in a woman's everyday life and elements in the urban landscape. Godard makes an assemblage of different sensations that are disconnected from the logic of linear narration—tree leaves, sun reflected on a red car, the honking sounds in the background.

Shot 4: Oppositions

Collage City is illustrated by several dozen paired images that regularly oppose two apparently irreducible conditions: object versus space, figure versus ground, positive versus negative, and so forth. One condition is doomed to be bad, the other good; rarely are they considered as two faces of the same coin, or as complementary as the proverbial socket and its plug. The authors' skill in selecting these oppositions is remarkable, as demonstrated by the juxtaposition of the *Unité* in Marseilles versus the Uffizi in Florence. The dialectics that are mapped out include space occupier versus space definer and solid versus void.

At one brief moment, however, a synthesis appears to be in sight:

> Neither object nor space fixation are, in themselves, any longer representative of valuable attitudes. The one may, indeed, characterize the 'new' city and the other the old: but [. . .] the situation to be hoped for should be recognized as one in which both buildings and spaces exist in equality of sustained debate.

Rowe's set of binary oppositions—solid versus void, Europe versus America, elitist versus populist, and so on—were understood by many of his followers as an "either/ or"; you had to choose your camp. For example, France in the 1970s was divided sharply between the "postmoderns" (who read Rowe) and the "Neo-Corbus" (who did not read very much). This either/or was not a dialectic but was simply a system of ideological exclusions. It was with Robert Venturi or, very differently, with Rem Koolhaas that oppositions such as elitist/populist ceased to exist and became "both/ and," and magazine titles went from *Oppositions* to *Assemblage*. Rowe included the following disclaimer, however: "We have identified two models; we have suggested that it would be less than sane to abandon either; and we are consequently concerned with their reconciliation, with, at one level, recognition of the specific and, at the other, the possibilities of general statement."

Rowe goes even beyond this refusal of one instead of the other by introducing other possible strategies: "crossbreeding, assimilation, distortion, challenge, response, imposition, superimposition, conciliation." *Collage City* is not a deconstructivist manual, but could there be a hidden discourse in Rowe's argument, despite himself and his many dedicated followers? I do not try to second-guess the writers' intention. I would rather suggest a "deconstructive" reading of their text, starting with the removal of its central crutch, the "binary" construction, and propose an alternative reading of urban history—namely, one based on abstract concepts and models, on multiple geometric configurations, all objectively valueless, each equal in its twentieth-century laser-like surgical precision. Namely, one term (say, *object*) is not better than the other (say, *space*).

Shot 5: Mutations

Godard's *Two or Three Things* is ambitious both as a documentary (it relates to the planning of the Paris region) and as pure research (as "a film where I [Godard] ask myself continuously what I am trying to do . . . the purpose is to observe a major mutation"). "For me to describe modern life, is to observe mutations," Godard says, asking whether today's city is made out of set pieces or instead of endlessly shifting parts, in which certainties are nothing but appearances, in a world that combines concrete blocks, fashion shows, endless construction sites, conspicuous consumption, desolate landscapes, holiday travel and leisure, *"terrains vagues,"* new media.[6]

Shot 6: *Plan Voisin*

One image has long struck my imagination—Rowe's famous juxtaposition of an aerial axonometric of Le Corbusier's *Plan Voisin* in Paris with an aerial photograph of the historical center of the Spanish city of Vitoria. Rowe's juxtaposition shows the city of (activating) objects against the city of (defining) spaces—that is, the defined spaces within Vitoria's dense built fabric versus the isolated objects of Le Corbusier's *Plan Voisin*. This image was one of several crucial triggers behind my 1982 Parc de la Villette competition entry.[7] In *Collage City*, the pair of images is inscribed as an opposition, with one of the terms being *wrong* and the other, *right*. As with many other oppositions by Rowe, such as Europe/America or high art/low art, it is constructed as either/or. Comparing different urban organizations during the early days of the competition, my sketches included the almost universally hated *Plan*

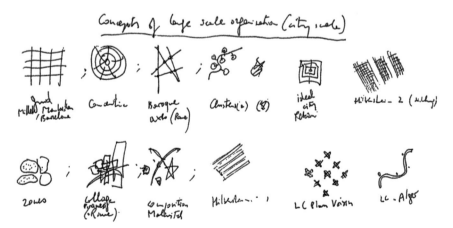

FIGURE 41 Bernard Tschumi, "Concepts of Large Scale Organization (City Scale)," La Villette, sketch (1982)

Credit: © Archives Bernard Tschumi

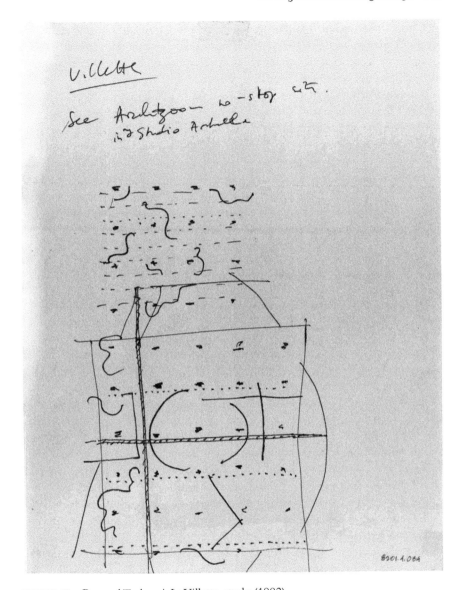

FIGURE 42 Bernard Tschumi, La Villette, study (1982)

Credit: © Archives Bernard Tschumi

Voisin. If so many people hated it, I thought, there might be something good about it. I was mostly interested in the conceptual rigor of its point grid as the ultimate anti-form, anti-function, anti-context statement. I also wanted to see how a system of spaces—here, a landscape—could be added to or superimposed on the system of objects represented by the point grid, meaning "spaces that define" together with "objects that activate."

I have often argued that the precedent for the La Villette point grid was my Joyce's Garden project (1976–77), which was based on a contemporaneous exercise given to my students at the Architectural Association in London. Others suggested that Archizoom's No-stop City or Peter Eisenman's 1978 project for Cannaregio in Venice might have played a role. In any case, Le Corbusier's respective point grids for his 1925 *Plan Voisin* in Paris and his 1964 Cannaregio Hospital project cannot be overlooked as the proper pedigree and common denominator between my 1982 Parc de la Villette, as well as Eisenman's 1978 Cannaregio scheme. Objects as activators: Is this a truly modern phenomenon, a generic or "canonical" model for modernist thought? Or is it an inescapable condition of all architectures or all cultures? At La Villette the binary object/space opposition eventually became a triad of "points/lines/surfaces" in the process of developing the competition scheme.

We will return to Le Corbusier.

Shot 7: Distortion of Type

Context is a given; the architect generally does not choose context but at best only redefines and qualifies it. In the process of discussing (and questioning) the absoluteness of pure types (the *cortile* or courtyard, the *galleria*, the *palazzo*) Rowe eventually addresses the messiness of contexts. Focusing mainly on the relation between context and formal types, he writes of "the ancient technique of deliberately distorting what is also presented as an ideal type," asking, "[H]ow is this building to be 'compromised' for use in a less than 'perfect' site?" This is an important consideration, yet Rowe drifts into an attack on functionalism, claiming its inability to conceive the deformation of ideal models. Of course, functionalism had little interest in ideal types, but to cite the doctrine of functionalism seems irrelevant here, precisely because it is a doctrine. However, "the deformation of ideal models" involves a critical statement. Rowe invokes the *de-formation*, the distortion of *form*.

In a powerful example, Rowe opposes the Hotel de Beauvais in Paris to the Villa Savoye in Poissy—unstable perimeter, stable interior (Beauvais) versus stable perimeter, unstable interior (Savoye). Behind the polemic and the argumentation, Rowe does not forget that this is never simple, and introduces further tension that challenges his own argument: a building can have both facade-figure (solid), and courtyard-figure (void). Again, Beauvais. Here, the connective tissue (which issues directly from context) becomes the "ground" (as *poché*) opposed to the facade/courtyard figures.

Shot 8: Definitions

For Rowe, deforming a type in order to make it fit the constraints of a site or respond to the requirements of a program is a formal operation. Let me here paraphrase Rowe in a more contemporary manner: Deforming a *concept*—in order to make it fit the *context* of a site or respond to the requirements of its *content*—is a strategic operation. But before I expand on the implications of this semantic shift, I must clarify some terms. I apologize to the reader for bringing up some well-known definitions regarding the use of the words *type* and *program*, as employed in their classical sense by Rowe, and of notions such as *concept, context*, and *content*.

> *Type*: "A type is an object from which anyone can conceive works of architecture that do not resemble each other." (Quatremère de Quincy, *Encyclopédie Methodique*, 1825) Similarly, a concept can be an idea from which anyone can design buildings that do not resemble one another.
>
> *Program*: An architectural program is a list of required utilities; it indicates their relations, but suggests neither their combination nor their proportion.[8]

Concept:

1 something conceived in the mind: thought, notion
2 an abstract or generic idea generalized from particular instances[9]

Context:

1 the interrelated conditions in which something exists or occurs: environment, setting[10]

Content:

1 something contained
2 the events, physical detail, and information in a work of art[11]

When Rowe talks about deforming a type in order to make it fit within a site or program, I call it "contextualizing a concept," that is, to place a concept in context.

Shot 9: *Contempt*

In reverse, can a context be conceptualized? In other words, can one interpret a context conceptually, can one form a concept out of a context? Let me use the following example.

Loosely based on Alberto Moravia's novel, Godard's 1963 film *Contempt* is an account of the disintegration of a relationship between a scriptwriter and his wife at a time when they are completing a film at the request of an American producer. Fritz Lang acts out his own part as the director. Starring Brigitte Bardot, the film was shot in part in the writer Curzio Malaparte's villa in Capri. It was Godard's first large-budget film. Except for the loose framework provided by Moravia's novel, the film has no "concept" to start with. But where would Godard take his film? Toward classical storytelling or formula plot, or was Godard interested in something quite different from a traditional narrative concept?

Godard was critical of Moravia's novel, which he considered "vulgar and cute." Nevertheless, he observed that "it is with this type of novel that one often makes good films . . . The subject of *Contempt* is people who look at each other and judge each other, and then are looked at, and judged by cinema."[12] Architecturally speaking, Moravia's novel is akin to a loose program that the architect can alter as he wishes. It is never a constraint. There is no preconceived type or form required, nor a precedent that must be adhered to. Godard's concept is a film about filmmaking, not only about the difficulty of making a film according to one's own vision of the world when faced with a producer's commercial demands but also about challenging the classical narratives and filming techniques of traditional cinema. Godard turns the novel into a film by conceptualizing this context (commercial demands and conventional narrative) in which he has to operate, challenging filmmaking and its conventions.

In a Brechtian manner, Godard separates cinema from real life and disregards conventional character motivations. He also disregards the usual rules of editing and continuity; situations are constructed and color serves to alter mood. Godard writes,

> The second part of the film will be entirely dominated by the point of view of colors by the deep blue of the sea, the red of the villa and the yellow of the sun. [. . .] The scenes of the film shot by Fritz Lang (the film in the film) will be more violent, more contrasting than in the rest of the film, like a painting by Matisse or Braque in the middle of a composition by Fragonard.[13]

Shot 10: Ideal or Functional Types?

Critical of ideal types, Rowe talks about their deformation. But what are ideal types, really? One could argue that ideal types became "form" only after they had been invented as "concept": a courtyard is a spatial and organizational *concept* before it becomes square, circular, or elliptical. The concept of the courtyard did not come out of nowhere, but necessarily began with a problem—for example, how to conceive of a place of encounter or a source of daylight in the middle of a dense, built-up area. Hence, the origin of the courtyard type may be argued to be functional in nature, at least until it becomes a concept, and eventually a type, when the functional or social reasons at its origin cease to be instrumental. And then, deformation: it is not a matter of deforming for the sake of form; indeed, it could be said more precisely that the ideal type often needs to be adapted to its many imperfect objective and subjective contexts—namely, it needs to be contextualized. Hence, "contextualizing concepts" cannot be reduced to formal strategy, even if it may occasionally be expressed through a deformation of types.

Shot 11: Villa Malaparte

Contextualizing concept, conceptualizing context? Can a context be conceptualized? This is different from starting from the dictionary of ideal types or received *"partis."*

The second part of *Contempt* takes place in Capri, at the Villa Malaparte, surrounded by wild rocks descending abruptly to the sea some hundred feet below it. In effect, Godard has made an experimental film that tests the limits of cinema in a house that tests the limits of architecture. But Malaparte's house is simultaneously surrealistic and utterly rational. It is also timeless. It is at once paradoxical and provocative, not unlike one of Godard's most extreme films about film. The house issues directly from its context, but not in a "contextualist" sort of way, in which integration and continuity are goals. The house could not be more contextual, and yet it makes no reference to Mediterranean or vernacular precedents.

Is the art of arriving at a concept a pure and abstract process? Often it is not; it is a messy, iterative labor of inclusion and exclusion, of testing and editing to get it exactly "right." So, too, was the design and construction of the villa—a fairly improvised process in which the original architect, Adalberto Libera, was dismissed or left of his own volition, friends gave contradictory advice, and local mason builders provided expertise, while the owner-designer aimed to "find himself" in the design of the house ("a casa come me") and searched for "an image of [his] nostalgia" for the prison in which he had recently been confined.[14] And, of course, there is the extraordinarily difficult site. All of these provide the context of the house and its making. There exists no pure type to emulate. And yet, paradoxically, the architecture gets purer and purer as construction unfolds. The addition of the inverted wedge-shaped stair during construction clinches the conceptual deal, as the "casa come me" now seems to "emerge from the rock to which it is married." Concept and material merge into one—"only stone, of the local kind, from which the cliff is made."[15]

Villa Malaparte conceptualizes a complex context made up of a rocky Mediterranean sea cliff on Capri and Malaparte's ego, turning the double presence of the scenery and of writer's persona into an intuitive and spectacular concept—"a naked portrait, with no ornament."[16] Born out of its context, the house cannot exist on another location or for a different client.[17] Even its interior bears the mark of an exceptional sense of circumstances, a sparse, uncompromising, and yet utterly sensual organization of spaces and materials. "*A ritratto di pietra*," said Malaparte; it was a symbol of modernity, with a taste for provocation, Malaparte's own portrait in stone.

Shot 12: Acropolis versus Forum

The chapter in *Collage City* called "Crisis of the Object: Predicament of Texture" displays an illustration of the figure-ground plan of Wiesbaden ca. 1900 on its penultimate page. (This image is also the cover of most editions of the book.) Printed on the facing page, the last sentence of the chapter appears to be one of few sentences in the book in italics, as if to suggest its profound significance. "Ultimately, in terms of figure-ground, the debate which is here postulated between solid and void is a debate between two models and, succinctly, these may be typified as acropolis and forum." The chapter ends.

An abrupt ending. That's it. Two large illustrations follow on the next double page, the Acropolis on the left and the Roman Forum on the right. But that is it—the end of the chapter. Do I read the Acropolis as the political left, the Forum, the political right?

The following chapter of *Collage City* is titled "Collision City and the Politics of Bricolage." Of the Acropolis, no more word is spoken. We read about gardens ("the garden as a criticism of the city"). We read about Hadrian's Villa, as opposed to Versailles. There are wonderful descriptions of hedgehogs versus foxes, with the hedgehogs concerned with the primacy of the idea—Plato, Dante, or Proust—and the foxes preoccupied with the diversity of stimulus—Aristotle, Shakespeare, Joyce. As for the architects, Mies van Der Rohe, Hannes Meyer, and Buckminster Fuller are hedgehogs, while Edwin Lutyens is a fox. Le Corbusier is "a fox disguised as a hedgehog for the purpose of public appearance." We also read about engineers versus *bricoleurs*, invoking Claude Lévi-Strauss's definition of the odd-job man who uses whatever is at hand to solve a problem, as opposed to the engineer who will devise specific tools to solve it. Eventually, we arrive at Rome, whose "physique and the politics . . . provide perhaps an example of collusive fields and interstitial debris." Clearly, Rowe is on the side of the fox and the *bricoleur*: "We prefer the complementary possibilities of consciousness and sublimated conflict."

Still, no further words about the Acropolis.

Shot 13: Le Corbusier's Sketches

In 1911 Le Corbusier visited the Acropolis, filling notebooks with sketches and reproducing one of them in *Vers une Architecture* (1923), commenting that the "generating idea" of the Acropolis allowed its edifices to be seen as if a block, "massed in the incident multiplicity of their plan." Later on in 1960, in a caption for one of his 1911 sketches, Corb writes, "The Parthenon appears (because it is outside the axis)." It is from this dissymmetry in relation to an autonomous object that Le Corbusier will derive the dynamics of his "*promenade architecturale*."[18]

Shot 14: Painting

Last chapter: "Collage City and the Reconquest of Time." Rowe draws on Karl Popper's theory of traditional values and his rejection of utopias, with an interesting quote about "Levi-Strauss's precarious balance: 'between structure and event, necessity and contingency, the internal and the external . . .'" Rowe again opposes two formulations that are distinct but interrelated: the utopian hedgehogs Marinetti, Gropius, or Hannes Meyer versus the *bricoleur* foxes Picasso, Joyce, and Proust. Collage is for the foxes. Rowe explains:

. . . because collage is a method deriving its virtue from its irony, because it seems to be a technique for using things and simultaneously disbelieving in them, it is also a strategy which can allow utopia to be dealt with as image, to be dealt with in *fragments* without our having to accept it in toto, which is further to suggest that collage could even be a strategy which, by supporting the utopian illusion of changelessness and finality, might even fuel a reality of change, motion, action and history.

Rowe uses analogies with literature, poetry, and art, even showing paintings and sculptures by Picasso. Nowhere is film—the twentieth-century century art *par excellence*—even mentioned. Rowe and Slutzky's transparency theory seems to be only "about" painting. This point is important, since in the late 1970s, when architecture reached the walls of art galleries, most architects of Rowe's generation were celebrating "drawing" and "painting." The next generation—Rem Koolhaas, Jean Nouvel, myself, and others—would use film instead of painting as its primary visual art connection.

And yet, no mention of the Acropolis.

Shot 15: Eisenstein at the Acropolis

In 1936 the filmmaker Sergei Eisenstein visited the Acropolis. Fascinated by the experience, he wrote a short text titled "Montage and Architecture," which he illustrated with diagrams by the architectural historian Auguste Choisy. Eisenstein described the Acropolis as an example of what montage could and might be. Moving past the temples and statuary, he experienced the highly organized visual collision of elements as an analogue to how filmmakers might cut shots or sequences of images and juxtapose them against one another. As he wrote in the same essay:

> The Greeks have left us the most perfect example of shot design, change of shot, and shot length (that is, the duration of a particular impression) . . . The Acropolis of Athens has an equal right to be called the perfect example of one of the most ancient films . . . It is hard to imagine a montage sequence more subtly composed, shot by shot, than the one that our legs create by walking among the buildings of the Acropolis.

What if Rowe's book had been called *Montage City*? Would it have recalled Eisenstein's "Montage of Attractions" (1923), Revolutionary Russia's battle cry? Could the calculated collision of shots used to trigger affects or emotions in the viewer be transposed in architecture? Defining several methods of montage, from metric to rhythmic to tonal to intellectual, Eisenstein argued that the juxtaposition of two independent shots could generate an idea.

Back to *Collage City*: The Acropolis never reappears. The powerful one-liner, the one-picture statement remains silent on its solitary rock. Contempt? Or an unfinished montage?

Last Shot

In that improbable meeting of Colin Rowe and Jean-Luc Godard, Le Corbusier and Sergei Eisenstein ("the chance meeting of the umbrella and the sewing machine on the dissecting table" of surrealist lore?), object and space, types and constraints, objective and subjective shots are meant to be inseparable, and architectural concept, programmatic content, and social context are interdependent.

Despite questioning the unitary and totalizing "modernist" ideologies of the 1920s and 1930s, *Collage City* describes a multiplicity of alternative urban strategies that are found throughout history. However, through Rowe's device of binary oppositions, the multiplicity gets lost and the modernist strategies are trashed, or so many of Rowe's contemporary followers thought. Still, *Collage City* is infinitely more complex than its apparent binary construction suggested to countless architects at the time who saw in it a tool to discredit and eradicate modernity so as to return to traditional, pre-twentieth-century historicist urban images.

Did Rowe and Koetter play on the ambivalence of the book's apparent thesis ("no to modernity, yes to historicity") in order to attract a large, conservative audience desperate for an alternative to the tough, progressive social plans of the "moderns"?

It is my contention that if Rowe and Koetter so carefully avoided any mention of the cinema—the archetypal art form of the twentieth century—and resorted instead to a painterly analogy, it is because their argument is based upon a deeply embedded belief that architecture and the city are the embodiment of permanence and stasis. Cinema is, by definition, about change and motion. Collage, in the mind of Rowe, is about space. Montage, as conceived in film, is about space *and* time.

So when Rowe speaks about Rome, it is almost always about conservative serenity and composure of forms, even when he speaks about the need for a contextual distortion of types. I would argue that it is no accident that the Acropolis is so carefully avoided, not only because, as Eisenstein demonstrates, it is a masterly dynamic montage, but also because montage suggests a society in constant flux and an architecture of uncertainty and conflict. Should one extend the demonstration to Rowe's political position, that is, whether Rowe was a conservative deeply mistrustful of the vagaries of progressive thought? I will let the reader decide.

If the dynamic and socially progressive dimension of "montage" may be absent from *Collage City*, this major work should not be reduced to a simple set of binary oppositions. It might be that the constant alternation of pre-modern vs. modern—meaning the good guys vs. the bad guys—is a form of alternating montage, comparable to parallel editing in cinema (a narrative dramatic device that is generally conceived by the scriptwriter). Could it be that Rowe pretended that he was advocating the triumph of the good guy (history), but could not help being fascinated by the bad guy (the modern)?

Notes

1 On this theme of Godard's film as it relates to Rowe, see also Anthony Vidler, "Two or Three Things I Know about Him," in *Any 7/8, Form Work: Colin Rowe*, guest ed. by R.E. Somol, September 1994: 44–47.

2 I am indebted to Alex Tschumi, who brought back to my attention the major role that architecture and the city have played in several of Jean-Luc Godard's films.

3 I only met Rowe "at a distance," from the back of the auditorium at the AA in London or at a party at the Institute for Architecture and Urban Studies in New York. I mostly met him through the filter of others—for example, through Bernhard Hoesli, my first architecture professor at the ETH in Zurich (who was also one of the so-called Texas Rangers and brought Rowe, Robert Slutzky, and John Hejduk to teach with him at the University of Texas at Austin), but also through Alvin Boyarsky in London and Peter Eisenman in New York, each of them influenced, in one way or another, by Rowe. Hoesli, Boyarsky, Eisenman, and Hejduk had all been important figures in my upbringing as an educator. But for me as a young architect, Rowe was a little like Clement Greenberg or Michael Fried for an art generation that came of age in the 1970s—they were simply not on our radar screen; neither friend nor foe.

4 All quotations are taken from Colin Rowe and Fred Koetter, *Collage City* (Cambridge, MA, and London: MIT Press, 1978)—a book which was essentially completed in 1973.

5 All Godard quotations are taken from Jean-Luc Godard, *Jean-Luc Godard par Jean-Luc Godard: articles, essais, entretiens* (Paris: Editions Pierre Belfond, 1968), 394–95.

6 Ibid., 392.

7 My competition entry report opposed four types of compositions: Palmanova, Campo Marzio, Camillo Sitte, and the Baroque Axes. The La Villette project intended to confront space and object in one single place, in a relation of conflict, indifference, or reciprocity.

8 Julien Guadet, *Eléments et théorie de l'Architecture*, cours professé à l'Ecole Nationale et Spéciale des Beaux-Arts, 4 vols, Paris 1901–04.

9 "Concept," in *Merriam-Webster's Online Dictionary*, accessed 15 March 2014, http://www.merriam-webster.com/dictionary/concept.

10 "Context," in *Merriam-Webster's Online Dictionary*, accessed 15 March 2014, http://www.merriam-webster.com/dictionary/context?show=0&t=1415854728.

11 "Content," in *Merriam-Webster's Online Dictionary*, accessed 15 March 2014, http://www.merriam-webster.com/dictionary/content.

12 Guadet, *Eléments*, 330.

13 Ibid., 331.

14 All quotes about the Casa Malaparte are taken from Marida Talamona, *Casa Malaparte* (New York: Princeton Architectural Press, 1992), 62.

15 Ibid., 85.

16 Ibid., 84.

17 Alternatively, we could dissociate content from context and say that the house is simultaneously concept (arrived through multiple iterations), context (the rocks, the sea, the sun, the period), and content (the writer Malaparte himself). Perhaps "concept, context, and content" is what architecture actually is.

18 See Jacques Lucan's *Composition, Non-Composition: Architecture et Théories, XIXe-XXe siècles* (Lausanne: Presses Polytechniques et Universitaires Romandes, 2009), 362.

Postscript

COMPARING COMPARISONS IN COLIN ROWE

Jonah Rowen

In conclusion to his essay "Robert Venturi and the Yale Mathematics Building Competition," Colin Rowe writes what seems to be a truism: "To be worthy of criticism a building must possess qualities."[1] Reading the essays collected in this book, one understands that the major concern in Rowe's work is precisely to identify those qualities and that identifying criteria for doing so is his greatest project. Whichever are the specific qualities of a given work that Rowe chooses to highlight, his uncanny ability to distill and to abstract works of architecture to one or another of their particular aspects is still impressive today. Where critical considerations of architecture can easily resort to broad generalities, Rowe's consistent capacity to isolate and interpret the singular attributes of specific works allowed him to draw minor but significant distinctions, avoiding the pitfalls of totalization.[2] An enduring part of Rowe's legacy, therefore, is his faculty of abstraction.

Abstraction in Rowe's writing can be seen most clearly in his continual use of comparison throughout his career. The works that Rowe brings together for analysis are shown to share at least one quality, which he masterfully draws out and focuses on; by temporarily divesting works of almost all of their properties, he isolates the relevant qualities of the works under consideration in order to make comparisons that would otherwise seem incongruous—like his equation of the Villa Malcontenta and the Villa Stein-de Monzie. Authors' intentions are routinely bracketed, and the social or economic of the histories of buildings are suppressed entirely.[3]

Although perhaps obvious, this recapitulation of Rowe's methods may be useful in order to consider his legacy and its continuing relevance. If, as Joan Ockman suggests, a large portion of Rowe's work was predicated on the disjunction between what modern architecture promised and what it could achieve, it is worth noting that contemporary architects no longer find the pretenses of utopia necessary to justify their projects.[4] Following the wide-ranging urban projects of architectural visionaries during the early part of the twentieth century, including those of Tony

Garnier, followers of Ebenezer Howard and the Garden City movement, Le Corbusier, Ernst May, and Martin Wagner (to list a few), architects' societal ambitions gradually decreased. The revivals of utopian architectural thought in the 1960s by Yona Friedman, Kenzo Tange, Constant Nieuwenhuys and Archigram—executed according to varying levels of sincerity—were subsequently parodied in the following decade by Archizoom ("No-Stop City"), Ettore Sottsass ("The Planet as Festival") and Rem Koolhaas, Madelon Vriesendorp and Elia Zenghelis ("Exodus, or the Voluntary Prisoners of Architecture" and "The City of the Captive Globe"). Anticipating a shift away from large-scale societal change in his 1959 essay "The Architecture of Utopia," Rowe treated the idea of utopia as a naïve ambition, focusing on the shapes that have been used to signify utopia historically and eschewing discussion of utopia itself (except to suggest its undesirability).[5] The 1973 addendum to that same essay concludes with the censure "Utopia, in any developed form, in its post-enlightenment form, must surely be condemned as a monstrosity . . . Utopia will persist—but should persist as a possible social metaphor rather than probable social prescription."[6] Architects have since heeded Rowe's condemnation, making an experiment like Paolo Soleri's ongoing Arcosanti project into a hopelessly anachronistic holdover from a more sincere era. Those interested in upholding architectural autonomy seem to have conceded that societal agency belongs to legislation, business and policy rather than architectural forms, even at their most carefully considered.[7] Architects have continued to attempt more pragmatic but accordingly piecemeal experiments in aspirational planning, but expectations for what architecture can accomplish have, to a large extent, been tempered.

Regardless of the particular politics embedded within one's approach to architecture, the significant portion of Rowe's legacy belongs to his methods. In other words, *what* Rowe's arguments were, is today less important than *how* he constructed them. Specifically, the emphasis he placed on the close scrutiny of architectural form may be useful for architects and critics today (and, accordingly, might imply a political position in its own right).[8] Beyond simply presenting works of architecture, Rowe's analytic mechanisms, including abstraction and comparison, force us to consider the means by which we look at architecture; since Rowe certainly did not invent these analytic tropes, their familiarity prompts one to ask exactly how he used them—as distinct from Wittkower's analyses, for example—and in turn how we might as well. Rather than being simply self-conscious, such methodological awareness is essential for any claim that architecture has a discourse or is a discipline at all.

A comparison of three examples of Rowe's methods will suffice to illustrate this point, despite his ironic warning: "[A]re not most comparisons and most analogies dangerous and foolhardy?"[9] The three primary examples to consider are the pairings of Andrea Palladio's Villa Malcontena and Le Corbusier's Villa Stein-de Monzie in Garches, Le Corbusier's *Unité d'Habitation* in Marseilles and Giorgio Vasari's Uffizi in Florence and Giuliano da Sangallo's Santa Maria delle Carceri in Prato and Antonio da Sangallo the Elder's San Biagio in Montepulciano.[10] These three examples, taken from various stages of his career, suggest a typology of his interests. Though provisional and incomplete, the system of classification proposed here could be used toward a further structural understanding of Rowe: a way of analyzing his analyses, as it were.

Rowe offers a rationale for each of these comparisons differently. In the first, Malcontenta/Garches, the two buildings "are superficially so entirely unlike that to bring them together would seem to be facetious."[11] In this case, the method of abstraction relies upon drawing an *equivalence*, given that Rowe implies that the buildings are high points of late Renaissance and early modern architecture, respectively. This is not unlike Le Corbusier's own incongruous juxtapositions, for instance the page in *Toward an Architecture* that pairs the Parthenon with the 1921 Delage Grand-Sport—each as exemplary products of its time.[12] The justification for the Unité/Uffizi comparison, on the other hand, is *oppositional*: one is the inversion of the other. This is only evident by means of abstractly considering the Unité as a solid and the Uffizi as a void, rhetorically corroborating the figure/ground technique Rowe and Koetter use throughout the pages of *Collage City*. In the last, Santa Maria delle Carceri/San Biagio, the comparison is *typological*; Rowe calls these two projects "members of the same species."[13] Both plans are based on a Greek cross, and Rowe tells us that he hardly needs to justify the comparison: "their differences are as startling as their similarities are evident."

The three comparisons differ regarding their respective methods of abstraction as well. Rowe makes the Malcontenta/Garches pairing plausible by reducing each building to lines, and then comparing those. The relationship between the Unité/Uffizi is established by abstracting the unité to a solid block and the Uffizi to a voided mold, suggesting that the two are fundamentally different types from one another. The equation of Santa Maria delle Carceri/San Biago has to do with solids and voids as well, but on the scale of walls rather than entire buildings; the building in Prato seems to be made of planes, whereas the one in Montepulciano is made of solids.

In some cases Rowe expresses a preference in favor of one building in the pair, and in others he remains impartial. In Malcontenta/Garches, for instance, he refrains from bias with the small exception of a few ambivalent adjectives, which remain non-preferential; for instance, the situation in Le Corbusier's work is "more complex" while also being "deeply perplexing." In this comparison, the two are analogous pieces of architecture, both of which are simply better than any derivative works of either, since the derivatives do not adhere to the same high mathematical standards considered in the article. In contrast, the Unité/Uffizi comparison is heavily weighted toward the latter project. Rowe and Koetter write explicitly that they have "bias[ed] the comparison," a preference that they explain through the argument that the architecture of that project resides as much in its inside space as in its outside. That is, whereas the Unité is a solid block whose architectural purview extends only as far as its exterior surfaces, the Uffizi is as much an urban container as it is a building with an inside of its own. In Santa Maria delle Carceri/San Biagio, however, the two churches are based on the same formal structure, so it is the difference of the thickness of the walls that is of consequence. Rowe's point echoes Le Corbusier's about Greek temples or cars once again: Santa Maria delle Carceri is the germinal, primitive type, whereas San Biagio is an evolved product of the standard established by Bramante in his work in Rome.[14]

In each case, the three pairs of buildings need to be transformed, reduced or distilled in order for Rowe to make his arguments about similarities and differences, and one could categorize all of Rowe's comparisons according to similar criteria. For instance, one could classify all of the comparisons that Rowe makes in which he exhibits a preference for one side over the other; in that regard, the juxtaposition of the Unité and the Uffizi is similar to that of the Bauhaus and the League of Nations project. In contrast, Rowe does not explicitly argue that either the Mies van der Rohe's Brick Country House or Michelangelo's Sforza Chapel is superior to the other, instead electing simply to point out features of each that allow him to describe them as centrifugal and centripetal, respectively.[15] One could draw a further distinction between either of the two previous comparisons and that of Le Corbusier's project for the Palace of the Soviets with Erik Gunnar Asplund's Stockholm Royal Chancellery in *Collage City*, which argues for a dialectical synthesis between the two projects.[16]

A complete list of the criteria on which Rowe bases his comparisons, and his resulting judgments, would constitute a catalogue of the "qualities" he uses to deem a building "worthy of criticism." The list would include the familiar terms in Rowe's lexicon, including centrifugal/centripetal, symmetry/asymmetry, character composition, horizontality/verticality, literal/phenomenal transparency, figure/ground, *contrapposto*, frontality, flatness/depth and so on. The telling part of this list, however, would not be the terms themselves, but the fact that each is an abstraction. That is, these imply a mode of looking at architecture apart from the physical reality of mortar and bricks, or even the physical reality of ink and paper. Much more than as attributes of any given building or another, they are ideas that exist *between* works. Neither ephemeral nor simply qualitative, taken together, this collection of abstract descriptors is the criteria for evaluating works as architecture, according to the disciplinary structures of architecture. Abstraction, then, is the process of detaching these qualities from specific instances of usage, thereby transforming them from properties of a specific object into architecture in general.[17]

In "Mannerism and Modern Architecture," Rowe refers to abstraction as a "mental order," a tendency that reveals more about its practitioners than the immediate object under consideration.[18] Reading that essay, in which Rowe interprets Renaissance abstraction as an inclination toward ideality and modernist abstraction as individual and insular, one is compelled to ask, "What 'mental order' does Rowe's abstraction presume, and how might one put those same tools to use today?" A tentative answer to this question would be that abstraction in Rowe is a mechanism for the deferral of reality: the agent for distilling a work of architecture to only the factors that are particular to that work, and discarding the aspects that pertain to lived experience of a work, or representations that attempt to simulate a work's experiential aspects. In this way, one is able to closely scrutinize architecture for its specifically architectural qualities, as distinct from the ones that are only manifest in the built versions of architecture. Reading Rowe, one is left with the impression that architecture is to be thought, not just experienced, in which case architecture's cultural efficacy lies in its ability to estrange itself from the habituation of everyday life. Confronted constantly by the realities that shape the production of architecture in the contemporary world (for instance, photorealism, economic realities, real-time technologies, etc.), one might, instead, focus one's attention on the potentials that processes of abstraction can reveal for architecture today.

Notes

1 Colin Rowe, "Robert Venturi and the Yale Mathematics Building Competition," in *As I Was Saying* vol. 2 (Cambridge, MA: MIT Press, 1996), 100. Incidentally, one might recall that O.M. Ungers built a project he called "Haus ohne Eigenschaften," after Robert Musil's *Man Without Qualities* (*Der Mensch ohne Eigenschaften*). Whereas Ungers's abstraction was entirely formal, and not formal*ist*—that is, Ungers's work *looks* abstract—the results of processes of abstraction in Rowe do not look like anything in particular.

2 As, for instance, laid out by Paul de Man: "no sequence of actual events or no particular subject could ever acquire, by itself, full historical meaning. They all become part of a process that they neither contain nor reflect, but of which they are a moment." De Man, "Genesis and Genealogy," *Allegories of Reading* (New Haven, CT: Yale University Press, 1979), 81.

3 This is what, presumably, has led many to appropriately apply the label "formalist" to Rowe. See, for instance, Joan Ockman, "Form Without Utopia: Contextualizing Colin Rowe," *Journal of the Society of Architectural Historians*, 57, no. 4 (December 1998): 450; K. Michael Hays, "Introduction" to an excerpt from *Collage City* in *Architecture Theory Since 1968* (Cambridge, MA: MIT Press, 1998), 89; "Form Work: Colin Rowe," ed. R.E. Somol, *ANY*, 7/8 (September 1994), especially R.E. Somol, "Oublier Rowe," 8–15, and Greg Lynn, "New Variations on the Rowe Complex," 38–43; Rosalind Krauss, "Death of a Hermeneutic Phantom," in *Peter Eisenman: Houses of Cards* (New York: Oxford University Press, 1987), 171–173; Daniel Sherer, "Le Corbusier's Discovery of Palladio in 1922 and the Modernist Transformation of the Classical Code," *Perspecta* 35 (2004), 20–39; and Pier Vittorio Aureli, "Architecture and Content: Who's Afraid of the Form-Object?," *Log* 3 (Fall 2004): 34.

4 "His [Rowe's] continuing theme has been the failure of the utopian project of modernism, the naive and tragic aspiration on the part of modern architects to construct the future of society through architecture." See Ockman, "Form Without Utopia," 449.

5 Rowe asks, rhetorically, "Now need we say that the state never can be turned into a work of art? That the attempt to do so is the attempt to bring time to a stop, the impossible attempt to arrest growth and motion? . . . For the work of art is not life; and nor, for that matter, is Utopia politics." Rowe, "The Architecture of Utopia," in *The Mathematics of the Ideal Villa and Other Essays* (Cambridge, MA: MIT Press, 1976), 212.

6 Ibid., 216.

7 In his essay "Critical of What? Toward a Utopian Realism," Reinhold Martin discusses the attenuation of radical political thought as it has been applied in architecture. See Martin, "Critical of What? Toward a Utopian Realism," *Harvard Design Magazine* 22 (Spring/Summer 2005): 1–5.

8 Such an argument would have to be developed in much more depth, but one might follow W.J.T. Mitchell's extrapolation in the essay "The Commitment to Form; or, Still Crazy after All These Years," in which he writes, "a commitment to form is also finally

a commitment to emancipatory, progressive political practices united with a scrupulous attention to ethical means. Insofar as formalism insists on paying attention to a way of being in the path rather than to where the path leads, it seems to me central to any notion of right action." See Mitchell, "The Commitment to Form; or, Still Crazy after All These Years," *PMLA* 118 (March 2003): 324.

9 Rowe, "Moneo's Spain," in *As I Was Saying*, vol. 2, 370. See also W. J. T. Mitchell, "Why Are Comparisons Odious?," *World Literature Today* 70 (Spring 1996): 321–24.

10 For these three comparisons, see, respectively, Rowe, "The Mathematics of the Ideal Villa," in *The Mathematics of the Ideal Villa and Other Essays*, 2–16; Rowe and Fred Koetter, "The Crisis of the Object: The Predicament of Texture," in *Collage City*, 68; and Rowe and Leon Satkowski, "Bramante & Leonardo," in *Italian Architecture of the 16th Century* (New York: Princeton Architectural Press, 2002), 2–4.

11 Rowe, "The Mathematics of the Ideal Villa," 3.

12 Le Corbusier, *Toward an Architecture*, trans. John Goodman (Los Angeles: Getty Research Institute, 2007), 181.

13 Rowe and Satkowski, *Italian Architecture of the 16th Century*, 3.

14 Bramante's relevant works in Rome include, notably, his plans for St. Peter's, the Tempietto, Santa Maria della Pace, the Palazzo Caprini and the choir at Santa Maria del Popolo, all of which rely heavily on stark masses and solidity. Regarding Santa Maria della Pace, Arnaldo Bruschi writes, "The eye, led along the perspective cross-axes, is drawn to the central piers but is halted when it reaches them; indeed, they send it back to the interior of the open space, to 'emptiness'. It is this open space that becomes the real protagonist of the architecture. . . ." See Arnaldo Bruschi, *Bramante* (London: Thames and Hudson, 1973), 74. Interestingly, though tangentially, the flatness that Rowe celebrated in Garches and in the "Transparency" articles would probably be distinguished from the flatness in Prato; yet it is exactly this quality that, Rowe argues, elevates Garches and the Palace of the League of Nations over the Bauhaus building at Dessau.

15 See "Mannerism and Modern Architecture," in *The Mathematics of the Ideal Villa and Other Essays*, 45–49.

16 See Rowe and Koetter, *Collage City*, 72.

17 Charles Sanders Peirce calls this process "hypostatic abstraction": "the abstraction which transforms 'it is light' into 'there is light here,' which is the sense which I shall commonly attach to the word abstraction . . . is a very special mode of thought. It consists in taking a feature of a percept or percepts (after it has already been prescinded from the other elements of the percept), so as to take propositional form in a judgment (indeed, it may operate upon any judgment whatsoever), and in conceiving this fact to consist in the relation between the subject of that judgment and another subject, which has a mode of being that merely consists in the truth of propositions of which the corresponding concrete term is the predicate. Thus, we transform the proposition, 'honey is sweet,' into 'honey possesses sweetness.' 'Sweetness' might be called a fictitious thing, in one sense. But since the mode of being attributed to it consists in no more than the fact that some things are sweet, and it is not pretended, or imagined, that it has any other mode of being, there is, after all, no fiction. The only profession made is that we consider the fact of honey being sweet under the form of a relation; and so we really can. I have selected sweetness as an instance of one of the least useful of abstractions. Yet even this is convenient. It facilitates such thoughts as that the sweetness of honey is particularly cloying; that the sweetness of honey is something like the sweetness of a honeymoon; etc." See Peirce, *The Collected Papers of Charles*

Sanders Peirce, vol. 4: *The Simplest Mathematics* (Cambridge, MA: Harvard University Press, 1958), §235.

18 "But it is clear too that, although working with a visual medium, the abstract art of today is working with a not wholly visual purpose. For abstraction presupposes a mental order of which it is the representative." Rowe, "Mannerism and Modern Architecture," in *The Mathematics of the Ideal Villa and Other Essays*, 40.

CONTRIBUTORS

Alan Colquhoun (1921–2012, England) received his degree in architecture from the Architectural Association (AA), London, in 1949. He taught at AA, Cornell, New York University, University College Dublin, The Polytechnic of Central London, l'École polytechnique fédérale de Lausanne, and Princeton University. As a practicing architect, he was co-founder, with John Miller, of Colquhoun + Miller + Partners (1961–1990). Colquhoun, according to Reyner Banham in *New Brutalism*, is "one of the guardians of the intellectual conscience of his generation of London architects"; he is author of several books including *The Oxford History of Modern Architecture* (2002), the seminal *Essays in Architectural Criticism* (1981), and *Modernity and the Classical Tradition* (1989), the latter two now jointly published as *Collected Essays in Architectural Criticism* (2008).

Peter Eisenman (b. 1932, United States) received degrees in architecture from Cornell, Columbia, and Cambridge universities—it was in England where he pursued doctoral studies. He has been awarded honorary Doctorates from the University of Illinois, Chicago; the Pratt Institute in New York; Syracuse University; and the Università La Sapienza in Rome. In 1967 he founded the Institute for Architecture and Urban Studies (IAUS) and its related journal *Oppositions*; Eisenman is currently the Charles Gwathmey Professor in Practice at the Yale School of Architecture. Before Yale, he taught at Cambridge, Princeton, Harvard, and Ohio State and was the Irwin S. Chanin Distinguished Professor of Architecture at The Cooper Union in New York City. His built work includes the Wexner Center for the Arts at Ohio State, the City of Culture of Galicia in Spain, and the Memorial to the Murdered Jews of Europe in Berlin. His most recent books include *Written into the Void: Selected Writings, 1990–2004* (2007) and *Ten Canonical Buildings, 1950–2000* (2008).

Bernhard Hoesli (1923–1984, Switzerland) received his architecture degree from the Eidgenössische Technische Hochschule Zürich (ETHZ) in 1944. He worked for Fernand Léger and later for Le Corbusier, being in charge of the Curutchet House (Argentina) and the Unité d'Habitation in Marseille (France). He taught at the School of Architecture at the University of Texas Austin with Colin Rowe, Robert Slutzky, and others as part of the so-called Texas Rangers from 1951 to 1959, when he joined the ETHZ to teach studio and later to found, along with Paul Hofer and Adolph Max Vogt, the Institute for the History and Theory of Architecture (gta). A tribute edition *Bernhard Hoesli: Collages* (2001) was edited by Christina Betanzos Pint, with contributions by Mark Jarzombek and John P. Shaw.

Rem Koolhaas (b. 1944, the Netherlands) studied at the Netherlands Film and Television Academy in Amsterdam, Cornell University, the Institute for Architecture and Urban Studies, and received his degree in architecture from the Architectural Association in London. A Professor in Practice of Architecture and Urban Design at the Graduate School of Design at Harvard University, Koolhaas founded with Elia and Zoe Zenghelis and Madelon Vriesendorp the Office for Modern Architecture (OMA 1975). Some of his most celebrated buildings are the Kunsthal in Rotterdam (1993), the Netherlands Embassy in Berlin (2003), the McCormick Tribune Campus Center at the Illinois Institute of Technology in Chicago (1997–2003), the Public Library in Seattle (2004), the Casa da Musica concert hall in Porto (2001–2005), and the headquarters, studio, and cultural center for China's national broadcaster, China Central Television (CCTV) in Beijing (2004–2009). He heads the work of both OMA and AMO—OMA's research branch, which operates in areas beyond the realm of architecture such as media, politics, renewable energy, and fashion. He has published *Delirious New York: A Retroactive Manifesto for Manhattan* (1978), *S,M,L,XL* (1995), *Content* (2003), and *Project Japan. Metabolism Talks . . .* (2011, with Hans Ulrich Obrist). Koolhaas has won several international awards including the Pritzker Architecture Prize (2000), the RIBA Gold Medal (2004), and the Golden Lion for Lifetime Achievement at the 2010 Venice Biennale. He was curator of the 14th International Architecture Exhibition at the Venice Biennale in 2014.

Léon Krier (b. 1946, Luxembourg) studied architecture at the University of Stuttgart, and later worked for Jim Stirling in London from 1968 to 1974; he was a founding Trustee of the New School for Traditional Architecture & Urbanism in Charleston. He is the architect of the Prince of Wales's model town of Poundbury in Dorset, England. Professor of Architecture and Town Planning at the Architectural Association and Royal College of Arts, London, and later Professor of Architecture at Princeton University and the University of Virginia, Krier was Davenport Professor at Yale University (1990–1991), returning again to Yale in 2002 as Eero Saarinen Professor. He is the recipient of the Berlin Prize for Architecture (1977), the Jefferson Memorial Gold Medal (1985), the Chicago American Institute of Architects Award (1987), and the European Culture Prize (1995). In 2003, he became the inaugural recipient of the Richard H. Driehaus Prize for Classical and Traditional

Architecture. His book *Architecture: Choice or Fate* (1998) has been published in eight languages and is the winner of the Silver Medal of the Académie Française. Krier has stated, "I am an architect, because I don't build."

Robert Maxwell (b. 1922, England) studied at Liverpool University, where he met Jim Stirling and Colin Rowe, and has combined a life of practice with teaching. As well as being a Partner in Douglas Stephen and Partners, he became Professor of Architecture at the Bartlett, then Dean of Architecture at Princeton University, and is now Emeritus Professor of Architecture at Princeton, and working in London. His written work engages the history, theory, and criticism of art and architecture: *New British Architecture* (1973); *Sweet Disorder and the Carefully Careless: Theory and Criticism in Architecture* (1993); *James Stirling, Michael Wilford and Associates: Buildings and Projects 1975–92* (1994); *Two Way Stretch: Modernism, Tradition and Innovation* (1996); *Frank O. Gehry: Individual Imagination and Cultural Conservatism* (1995); and *New English House* (2005).

Emmanuel Petit (b. 1973, Luxembourg) studied architecture at the ETH in Zurich, and received his PhD in history and theory of architecture from Princeton University. He has taught at Yale, Harvard, and the Massachusetts Institute of Technology as associate and visiting associate professor, and is currently Sir Banister School of Architecture Fletcher Visiting Professor at the Bartlett School of Architecture in London. He is author of *Irony, or The Self-Critical Opacity of Postmodern Architecture* (2013); editor of *Philip Johnson: The Constancy of Change* (2009); and editor of *Schlepping Through Ambivalence: Writings on An American Architectural Condition* (2011)—all published by Yale University Press. He is cofounding partner of EPISTEME Architects.

Jonah Rowen (b. 1986, United States) is a PhD student in the history and theory of architecture at Columbia University. He studied architecture at Yale and Carnegie Mellon University and has taught at the Southern California Institute of Architecture. He is a founding editor of the architectural journal *Project* and has published essays in *Log, Pidgin,* and *Fulcrum*.

Robert Slutzky (1929–2005, United States) was a painter, a writer, and an educator who studied at Grand Central School of Art in New York; the University of California, Los Angeles; the Arts Students League; and The Cooper Union School of Art. He received art degrees from the Yale School of Art with Josef Albers, Stuart Davis, Jose de Rivera, Burgoyne Diller, and Ad Reinhardt (BFA, 1952; MFA, 1954). He taught at the University of Texas, Austin; Pratt Institute, Brooklyn; School of Architecture and School of Art, The Cooper Union; and the Department of Fine Arts, University of Pennsylvania. Slutzky coauthored "Transparency: Literal and Phenomenal" with Colin Rowe.

Bernard Tschumi (b. 1944, Switzerland) received his degree in architecture from the ETH in Zurich in 1969. He taught architecture at the Architectural Association in London, Princeton University, and The Cooper Union in New York. He was dean of the Graduate School of Architecture, Planning and Preservation at Columbia University from 1988 to 2003. He is the winner of many international competitions, such as the Parc de La Villette (Paris, 1983) and the new Acropolis Museum (Athens, 2008). A member of the College of Fellows of the American Institute of Architects, Tschumi was awarded France's Grand Prix National d'Architecture (1996) as well as numerous awards from the American Institute of Architects and the National Endowment for the Arts. He is an international fellow of the Royal Institute of British Architects in England and a member of the Collège International de Philosophie and the Académie d'Architecture in France, where he has been the recipient of distinguished honors that include the rank of Officer in both the Légion d'Honneur and the Ordre des Arts et des Lettres. The many books devoted to Tschumi's writings and architectural practice include the four-part *Event-Cities* series (1994, 2000, 2005, 2010), *The Manhattan Transcripts* (1981, 1994), *Architecture and Disjunction* (1994), and the monograph *Tschumi* (2003). The Centre Pompidou exhibited a retrospective on Tschumi's work in 2014.

O. Mathias Ungers (1926–2007, Germany) received his degree in architecture from the Technische Hochschule Karlsruhe, Germany, in 1950. A professor and Dean of the Architecture Department at the Technische Universität Berlin and chairman at Cornell, he also taught at Harvard University; University of California, Los Angeles; University of Applied Arts in Vienna; and the Kunstakademie in Düsseldorf. In the 1960s and 1970s, Ungers took part in numerous competitions, in particular for the student accommodation at TH Twente, Enschede (1964); Tegel Flughafen, Berlin (1966); urban restructuring of Berlin's Tiergarten quarter (1973); the new building of Wallraf-Richartz Museum in Cologne (1975); and the Bremen University complex (1977). In the 1980s he orchestrated the construction of the new exhibition hall on the Frankfurt fairgrounds (1980–1984), the Alfred Wegener Institute for Polar Research in Bremerhaven (1980–1984), the Baden State Library in Karlsruhe (1980–1991); and the organization of the Architecture Museum in Frankfurt (completed in 1984). His many awards included the "Bund Deutscher Architekten" prize, the "Rhenan" award and the "Grosser Verdienstkreuz des Verdienstordens der Bundesrepublik Deutschland." His publications include *Entwerfen mit Vorstellungsbildern, Metaphern und Analogien. Anmerkungen zu einem morphologischen Konzept, in: Architektur 1951–1990* (1991); *Morphologie. City Metaphors* (1982, 2011); *Die Thematisierung der Architektur* (1983, 2009); and *The Dialectic City* (1997).

Anthony Vidler (b. 1941, England) received his professional degree in architecture from Cambridge University in England, and his doctorate in history and theory from the TU Delft in the Netherlands. A historian and critic of modern and contemporary architecture, he taught at The Cooper Union, where he was dean from 2001 through 2013; at Princeton University from 1965 to 1993, serving as the William R. Kenan Jr. Chair of Architecture, the Chair of the PhD Committee, and Director of the Program in European Cultural Studies at Brown from 2013 to 2014; and as The Vincent Scully Visiting Professor of Architectural History at Yale since 2014. In 1993 he took up a position as professor and Chair of the Department of Art History at University of California, Los Angeles, with a joint appointment in the School of Architecture from 1997. He has received awards and prestigious fellowships from, among others, the Guggenheim Foundation, the National Endowment for the Humanities, the Getty Center for the History of Art and the Humanities, and the Canadian Centre for Architecture. A Fellow of the American Academy of Arts and Sciences, he received the architecture award from the American Academy of Arts and Letters in 2011. Vidler's many publications include *The Writing of the Walls: Architectural Theory in the Late Enlightenment* (1987), *Claude-Nicolas Ledoux: Architecture and Social Reform at the End of the Ancien Regime* (1990, Henry-Russell Hitchcock Award), *The Architectural Uncanny: Essays in the Modern Unhomely* (1992), *Warped Space: Architecture and Anxiety in Modern Culture* (2000), *Histories of the Immediate Present: The Invention of Architectural Modernism* (2008, with a chapter on Colin Rowe), and *Scenes of the Street and Other Essays* (2011).

IMAGE CAPTIONS AND CREDITS

(Book Cover Image) Rainer Jagals, Untitled, ink on paper, 26 x 19 cm (1967)

Credit: Courtesy Galerie Strecker, Rainer Jagals, exhibition catalogue, Dezember 1967–Februar 1968, Berlin

Portrait of Colin Rowe (February 1980)

Credit: © Rosa Feliu Atienza, Barcelona

FIGURE 1 Stirling & Wilford, Staatsgalerie, Stuttgart (1977–84)

Credit: © Richard Bryant; Courtesy ARCAID (Stirling 47-890-1)

FIGURE 2 *Architectural Review*, page spread, March 1956:"Le Corbusier's Chapel and the Crisis of Rationalism" (Ronchamp, France), by James Stirling

Credit: Courtesy of Architectural Review, London

FIGURE 3 Le Corbusier,Villa Schwob, photograph of front façade with blank panel

Credit: © F.L.C. / ADAGP, Paris / Artists Rights Society (ARS), New York 2014

FIGURE 4 Casa Cogollo, main facade,Vicenza; attributed to Andrea Palladio (1559)

Credit: Courtesy Centro Internazionale di Studi di Architettura Andrea Palladio,Vicenza

FIGURE 5 *Battle of Cascina*, after Michelangelo by Bastiano da Sangallo (ca. 1542)

Credit: By permission of Viscount Coke and Trustees of the Holkham Estate. Photograph:The Courtauld Institute of Art, London

FIGURE 6 Michelangelo,Vestibule of Laurentian Library, Florence (1525–71)

Credit: © Massimo Listri, Florence

FIGURE 7 Nicholas Hawksmoor, Proposition IV for Queen's College, street front, Oxford

Credit: Courtesy of The Provost and Fellows of the Queen's College, Oxford

FIGURE 8 Giuseppe Terragni, Novocomum Apartment Building, Como, Italy (1927–1929)

Credit: © John Hill

FIGURE 9 Le Corbusier, Sainte Marie de La Tourette, Éveux, France (1956–60)

Credit: © Cemal Emden, Istanbul

FIGURE 10 Le Corbusier, Sainte Marie de La Tourette, Éveux, France (1956–60)

Credit: © Miroslava Brooks

FIGURE 11 Peter Carl, Barbara Littenberg, Judith Di Maio, Steven Peterson, and Colin Rowe, "Roma Interrotta" contribution, Sector VIII of Nolli map of Rome from 1748 (1978)

Credit: Courtesy Steven Peterson and Barbara Littenberg

FIGURE 12 Cover of *Collage City* (1978)

Credit: Courtesy of MIT Press, Cambridge

FIGURE 13 Rainer Jagals, Hommage à O.M.U. (1967)

Credit: Courtesy Galerie Strecker, Rainer Jagals, exhibit catalogue, Dezember 1967–Februar 1968, Berlin

FIGURE 14 Rainer Jagals, Untitled, 30 × 19 cm (1967)

Credit: Courtesy Galerie Strecker, Rainer Jagals, exhibit catalogue, Dezember 1967–Februar 1968, Berlin

FIGURE 15 Rainer Jagals, Necropolis, isometric, 90.5 × 138 cm (1967)

Credit: Courtesy Galerie Strecker, Rainer Jagals, exhibit catalogue, Dezember 1967–Februar 1968, Berlin

FIGURE 16 Spiegel Cover 24/1967, "The Revolting Students of Berlin"

Credit: SPIEGEL 24/1967

FIGURE 17 O.M. Ungers, Urban Park with Representation Villas near Görlitz Train Station (1977)

Credit: With the permission of of Ungers Archiv für Architekturwissenschaften UAA, Cologne. From: O.M. Ungers. *The City in the City: Berlin: A Green Archipelago* (1977)

FIGURE 18 Cover page of *Rational Architecture: The Reconstruction of the European City* (1978)

Credit: Courtesy of Archives d'Architecture Moderne, asbl, Brussels

FIGURE 19 O.M. Ungers, Grünzug-Süd

Credit: Courtesy of Ungers Archiv für Architekturwissenschaften UAA, Cologne

FIGURE 20 Léon Krier, *Difficult Access to O.M.U.* (1975)

Credit: © Léon Krier

FIGURE 21 Rainer Jagals, Cityspace Fantasy/Vision (1967)

Credit: Courtesy Galerie Strecker, Rainer Jagals, exhibit catalogue, Dezember 1967–Februar 1968, Berlin

FIGURE 22 Léon Krier, Labyrinth City, project. Aerial perspective and section (1971). Ink with gouache on paper, 11 5/8 × 8 1/4 in. Gift of The Howard Gilman Foundation. (12.13.2000) The Museum of Modern Art, New York, NY, USA.

Credit: © Léon Krier (1946–); Digital Image © The Museum of Modern Art/Licensed by SCALA / Art Resource, NY

FIGURE 23 Léon Krier, Untitled (1973)

Credit: © Léon Krier

FIGURE 24 Léon Krier, From L.K. To C.R. (1975)

Credit: © Léon Krier

FIGURE 25 Rem Koolhaas, from "Berlin Wall as Architecture" photo series (ca. 1971)

Credit: © OMA; Office for Metropolitan Architecture; Heer Bokelweg 149, 3032 AD Rotterdam, Netherlands; www.oma.eu

FIGURE 26 Alfred Ziethen Verlag postcard of Berlin from Rem Koolhaas's "Berlin Wall as Architecture" photo series (ca. 1971)

Credit: © Alfred Ziethen Verlag; Courtesy OMA; Office for Metropolitan Architecture; Heer Bokelweg 149, 3032 AD Rotterdam, Netherlands; www.oma.eu

FIGURE 27 O.M. Ungers, German Embassy to the Vatican in Rome, competition project (1965)

Credit: Courtesy of Ungers Archiv für Architekturwissenschaften UAA, Cologne

FIGURE 28 Walter Gropius, Bauhaus, Dessau (1925–26)

Credit: © Burcin Yildirim, Istanbul

FIGURE 29 Le Corbusier, Villa Stein de Monzie (1926–28)

Credit: © Ralitza Petit

FIGURE 30 Le Corbusier, Villa Stein de Monzie, axon (1926–28)

Credit: © F.L.C. / ADAGP, Paris / Artists Rights Society (ARS), New York 2014

FIGURE 31 Cover to Sigfried Giedion's *Bauen in Frankreich* (1928)
Credit: Courtesy Klinkhardt & Biermann Verlag, München

FIGURE 32 John Hejduk, Wall House 1: Worm's eye view (1968–77). Reprographic copy, 89 × 92.5 cm
Credit: Courtesy of John Hejduk fonds, Collection Centre Canadien d'Architecture / Canadian Centre for Architecture, Montréal, DR1998:0077:036

FIGURE 33 Robert Slutzky, Homage to Bach, sketch (1973)
Credit: Courtesy Joan Ockman

FIGURE 34 Robert Slutzky, Homage to Bach, painting (1973–74)
Credit: Courtesy Joan Ockman

FIGURE 35 Le Corbusier et Pierre Jeanneret, Pavillon Suisse, Cité internationale universitaire, Paris (1929–33)
Credit: © F.L.C. / ADAGP, Paris / Artists Rights Society (ARS), New York 2014

FIGURE 36 "Rowe's Ghost"; Amtrak train ticket stubs with uncanny name confusion: "Rowe" instead of "Slutzky" (2001)
Credit: Courtesy Joan Ockman

FIGURE 37 Le Corbusier, League of Nations, Geneva (1927)
Credit: © F.L.C. / ADAGP, Paris / Artists Rights Society (ARS), New York 2014

FIGURE 38 Le Corbusier, Villa Curutchet, perspective drawing of front facade, La Plata, Argentina (1949–53); Hoesli worked on this project while employed in Le Corbusier's office.
Credit: © F.L.C. / ADAGP, Paris / Artists Rights Society (ARS), New York 2014

FIGURE 39 Mark Jarzombek, diploma thesis at the ETH in Zurich under Bernhard Hoesli, plan (1979–80)
Credit: © Mark Jarzombek

FIGURE 40 Mark Jarzombek, diploma thesis at the ETH in Zurich under Bernhard Hoesli, model (1979–80)
Credit: © Mark Jarzombek

FIGURE 41 Bernard Tschumi, La Villette, concept sketch (1982)
Credit: © Archives Bernard Tschumi

FIGURE 42 Bernard Tschumi, La Villette, study (1982)
Credit: © Archives Bernard Tschumi

INDEX

Note: Page numbers with *f* indicate figures.